DATE DUE

NOV 2 3 1983		
10-12-93		
12-9-94		
10-13-95		
11-3-95		
10-9-97		
8-6-98		

CHARGE IT

Charge It

Inside the Credit Card Conspiracy

Terry Galanoy

G. P. Putnam's Sons
New York

The author wishes to express appreciation for use of material from:
ACLU Privacy Report; American Banker, May 24 and 29, 1971 issues; the
Associated Press; *Banking,* reprinted by permission from the
September 1977 issue, copyright © 1977 by the American Bankers
Association; *Dun's Review,* reprinted with permission, June and
September 1978 issues, copyright © 1978, Dun & Bradstreet
Publications Corporation; the Los Angeles *Times; The Nilson Report;*
and *Privacy Journal,* Washington, D.C.

Library of Congress Cataloging in Publication Data

Galanoy, Terry.
    Charge it.

    1. Bank credit cards. 2. Credit cards.
I. Title.
HG1643.G34   332.7'6   80-18954
ISBN 0-399-12555-8

PRINTED IN THE UNITED STATES OF AMERICA

Dedication

As of publication date, the author *owed* $2100 to a dentist, $54.60 to a storage company, $500 for car insurance, $102.70 to the telephone company, $403.02 to department stores—and this book to Devon.

Credit Where Credit Is Due

A number of legislators, consumer advocates, computer experts, economists, journalists, bankers, and card-carrying members of the Great Credit Society contributed material for this book. Some gladly said that I could use their names. Others asked to be spared the credit and the attendant fear of losing their professional or social relationships with the financial industry and its people. All, however, were agreed that it was time for a book like this and contributed willingly, eagerly, and plentifully to these pages.

I would like to thank various executives of the Visa and MasterCard organizations, Spencer Nilson, the American Bankers Association, several individual bank officers, and other financial people for supplying me with interviews or data, despite a collective sneaking suspicion that this book might be unflattering to the card business. I would like to thank Kimberly Wulfert for her unstinting research and her investigative-journalism activities, and Christyne Stanford for helping to organize the manuscript. I am also grateful to Bill Flaxman, who helped get this project off the ground by getting me back to earth. And, most of all, I would like to thank my agent, Julie Coopersmith, who seems to devote 100% of her energies for only 10% of the proceeds; and an encouraging, enthusiastic editor named Diane Reverand and G. P. Putnam's Sons for their partnerships in helping to bring the crucial information in this book to all of you.

T. G.

Contents

CHARGE IT

Foreword

This book covers trillions of dollars, millions of card carriers and merchants, thousands of financial institutions, hundreds of bankers, tens of years, and one basic theme: the terrifying certainty of an all-controlling system called Lifebank—in our lifetime.

This is not a book of numbers, and I have deliberately kept them at a minimum. However, in juggling the myriad numerical mazes of transactions, volumes, purchasing powers, outstandings, accounts, cards, sales slips, transactions, balances, credits, and other measurements used in the credit and card industry, there has been an intense dedication to reporting these figures accurately. References employed were my personal experience plus annual reports, speeches, articles, numerical abstracts, papers, surveys, studies, and articles all prepared for or by various financial organizations or individuals involved with this field. Some of the information about credit-by-card is carefully guarded and deliberately confined to highly restricted files, to documents marked "confidential," and to top-executive-only communications. The task of unearthing this material is so difficult that one congressman, even with his powers of disclosure and subpoena, said, "As I go deeper into the credit card industry, I am beginning to find out the industry itself doesn't know too much about the credit card industry."

That is what that industry would like congressmen and others to believe. Actually, the credit card (especially the bank card) industry is one of the most carefully researched, constantly monitored, continually audited businesses in existence. If seeming confusion and lack of precise up-to-date figures seem to be modus moneymen, that is deliberate. With careful planning, with manipulated calculations, with involuted figuring, with creative categorization, the bank card industry has cleverly kept its scope, its penetration, its influence, and especially its profits fairly well disguised and quiet.

These pages contain the most complete compilation of information about the bank card industry ever assembled in one general-interest book. If, here and there, some of the numbers do not agree, it is because the bankers did not agree, or deliberately changed or disguised facts to show only the results they desired made public. In these areas of dispute, I have attempted to show all sources. Some totals mentioned in the text are for all credit cards and some are for bank cards alone, and that difference is marked wherever it seemed necessary for clarification. For simplicity, here, the total sales volumes for bank cards include cash advances, which is the accepted method of overview reporting in that industry.

But, as I said, this is not a book about numbers, but about the buying and selling of bank cards, of credit, of debt, of inflation, of Lifebank . . . and the buying and selling of you.

1

The Plastic Explosive

PLASTIC IS A material which can be formed, shaped, plied, and impressed. It can be deformed continuously and permanently in any direction, molded to go any way the pressure wants it to go.

That's the way your Visa and MasterCards are molded to do what the bankers want them to do.

That's also the way you are being pressured to do what the bankers want *you* to do.

Which is the real plastic—your Visa or MasterCard, or you?

Like those cards, you are being formed, shaped, plied, impressed. You are also being deformed continuously and permanently to go in the direction the pressure of the money-men want you to go.

Where they're taking you is to a totally different kind of economic society in which you will have little or no privacy, in which your income and everything you own will be under their control, in which you will be told what you can have and what might not be good for you, and in which millions and millions of people literally might not be able to survive.

It is down the road a piece, but not very far. Parts of it are operating right now.

Let's call it *Lifebank*. If you have a salary, an income, anything of value, you will have an account in it. That account will contain your paychecks, savings, dividends, stocks, bonds, equity in your car and home, the cash value of your furs and jewelry, of your life-insurance policy, royalties, and everything else you own; all of your assets in one neat, efficient, computer-controlled account. Everything you earn, inherit, win, or find will be automatically deposited in the account. That account, of course, will be located in a computer controlled completely by one or more banks or financial organizations.

You will be completely dependent upon Lifebank. Its computer will take a searching look at what you make and what you have, and will give you a personal credit rating. That rating will be reviewed regularly; go up when you get a raise or win a sweepstakes, go down when you lose your job or don't get that Christmas bonus. The Lifebank computer will take all of that tiresome paperwork out of your life. It will automatically and electronically pay your house mortgage or rent, car payment, insurance, utilities, telephone and other set expenses, and also make all deductions for disability, income tax, social security, and other regular obligations. What is left over is where you might get a little freedom. You can choose to put that surplus *value* (since your assets are made up of more than cash) into banker-approved investments, more insurance, and other places the controlling bankers feel are secure. Your day-to-day operating expenses will be handled by an account-within-the-account, and you will be assigned a formula, based on total value, on what you will be allowed for food, for entertainment, for travel, for clothing, for furnishings, for gifts.

To see where you are at any time, you can use a bank card or some other identification device in your home communications center. It will light up with your Lifebank statement. Included will be the condition of your holdings, your deposits, deductions, what you owe, and what payments are coming up soon. Should you decide to buy that little piece of retirement property in Arizona or an expensive new car, Lifebank will tell you whether the bankers feel you can afford it, whether they will lend you money on it, and what you own that will be used as ransom on the loan. If you are financially stable, that new car or Arizona down payment will be yours at a handsome interest rate. The computer will make sure that the loan is repaid by putting electronic liens against your holdings. If you borrow too much against your stocks, however, and can't repay on time or with enough money, these stocks will automatically be removed from your electronic account and be taken over by the bank. You will have no way to hide your assets from the organizations to which you owe money; no more hidden socks, no more cash caches under the Sealy. Your money or value will be banker-programmed and electronically controlled in the name of efficiency, cost controls, and other advantages the bankers will sell to you as benefits, but are essential to them for maximum control to make maximum profits.

You will be a CPA's delight and a financier's pride and joy; a profitable, dependable, fiscally sound, paid-up citizen even if they have to destroy your freedom and even your life to do it.

Your life? The gruesome fact is that if for some reason you had no Lifebank, you would have no credit. Since credit will control close to 100% of all buying at that time (even coins will be bought from vending machines with a plastic card), and since checking accounts will have been discontinued and cash made obsolete by Lifebank, you won't be able to buy anything, probably not even food. Except for relatives, government handouts, the kindness of strangers, missions, the Red Cross, and Salvation Army kitchens, you could literally starve to death.

If you are not a valid Lifebank member, you will not exist. That will come about because government officials will also be motivated to simplify, to get more efficiency, to cut governmental costs. To do that, you will become a code or a number. The same group of digits will identify you at birth, become part of your school records, your military-service papers, your employment sheets, your driver's license, Social Security, and Lifebank buying device. If the officials at Lifebank decide to drop you, the inter-tied computers will magnetically erase that number. Although you may be alive and hearty and walking around the streets, you will have been effectively "liquidated."

Science fiction? Science, yes. Fiction, no.

George Orwell's notorious character "Big Brother" from the book *1984* will actually turn out to be Big Banker; all-seeing, all-knowing, all-controlling, capable of destroying any resistance.

The bankers are already putting that Lifebank system into place.

Dee Hock, longtime president of BankAmericard and, later, the Visa system, the bank card's most aggressive and imaginative force, recently said, "The shift to primary reliance on the Visa name, coupled with the redesign of the card, has created options ranging from card accessing deposits [checking and savings accounts], mortgage equities, investments, and cash value of life insurance."

The "name" reliance he referred to was a carefully planned step-by-step program initiated by Visa to remove any reference to the words "credit," "debit," "bank," "card," and "charge" from that device. Visa's advertising began to sell the "most widely recognized *name* in the world." And Hock added, "[It] will be synonymous with worldwide financial services."

"Worldwide financial services." Translation: Lifebank. The computer people use the word "capture" to describe what the machine is doing when it takes data from another source. Capture is also what the bankers plan to do to us. The machinery today handles the myriad, complex details of the current 600 million credit cards of all types which are in circulation and the 7 billion transactions involved in spending some $300 billion.

Nor is Visa alone in this drive to put us all in line by putting us all on line. In explaining its 1980 name change from Master Charge to MasterCard, a spokesman of that organization said, ". . . MasterCard . . . is becoming a system for universal transactions. For banking needs and services." And, "We're laying the groundwork for the day when a card is really a bank in your pocket and the brick and mortar branch on the corner becomes an automated teller." An automated teller is that unmanned computer-controlled machine which can do just about everything a live bank teller can do except think and reason. If you are not on the computer or if the computer has specific instructions for handling your account, no amount of pleading with the lifeless teller is going to get you cent one, even if you're dying of malnutrition while punching its non-responsive keys.

Lifebank. That's where the bankers are going. That's where

they're taking you. And you helped them, you encouraged them, you voted for Lifebank and total control of your existence every time you used a credit card, especially the bankers' devices, Visa and MasterCard. Think about it. Today's international maze of complex electronic communications is already in place. It is so advanced that it takes only four seconds to get an okay from New York for you to buy something in Milan. The electronic controls are already there and are being reinforced with satellite signals, photoconductors, high-speed printers, optical readers, lightwave communications, and other information systems to control your "value."

In addition, think about how nearly everything you own is already in a bank. Your savings account, checking account, mortgage, personal loans, are part of the bank's everyday operations. Your jewelry, stocks, T-bills, insurance papers, are probably already in a safe-deposit box. All the bank has to do is collect your various belongings and put them into one central computer file which adds up value of the different items. That value will be symbolized on a plastic card (or some other identifying device) which will become an additional "convenience" for you. Instead of carrying up to twenty credit cards, that one card will replace your Visa, MasterCard, Sears, Penney, Texaco, American Express, Standard Oil, and other plastic rectangles you now carry around.

Initially, at month's end when the bills come in, you'll have the option of deciding which account pays what bill. You might use your savings account to pay for entertainment and clothing, interest on your investments to pay your mortgage or car lease, a small loan against your T-bills to pay for a new suit. Later, when you've been house-broken to that system, the rules will change and your options will disappear. Instead, the computer will make all of those decisions for you in order to keep you financially stable, and more importantly, to make the maximum amount of profits for the banks.

The advertising for Visa, for example, has been preparing you for these changes. It was cleverly constructed to make you believe it was all your idea. "You're growing and we're keeping up with you," soothed and assured the clever little jingle. "We just want to be of service," the bankers jollied us along.

It is already too late to do much about the system which has prepared us for the unthinkable Lifebank. The bank card system composed of Visa (also as BankAmericard) and Master-Card (also as Master Charge) has totally and forever changed the way we buy, trade, and sell. So complete and total a change is it that, worldwide, about 3 million merchants not only accept but also welcome and encourage use of the 155 million bank cards. Card holders increased 60% between 1974 and 1980. In the United States alone, more than 120 million people pack anywhere from one to a dozen bank cards, and two-thirds of them owe card money to the banks at any one time.

Some years, the bank cards have grown 35%, 40%, even up to 300% over the year before. In 1981, an estimated $110 billion will be spent with bank cards. One bank-card observer conservatively estimates that by 1985, there will be 700 million credit cards around and that some 255 million of them will be bank cards. That will be more than one for every man, woman, and child in the United States, although they won't be distributed that way. By that year, more than 85 million Americans will be carrying "financial" cards (the more complete Lifebank-type bank card), and some financial experts say that number will be just about the saturation point of financially sound adults in the United States. That means Lifebank could become a reality by 1985, perhaps sooner. Today, there are already some financial institutions, some savings-and-loan associations that will issue you one or more Visa cards that work against your central account exactly as Lifebank will work. The dream of the bankers is ready to become a nightmare for the rest of us.

The most ironic twist is that originally the bankers didn't want the bank credit card. It was developed as a device to get you from Point C to Point E without too much resistance on your part. Point C is checks. Bankers wanted to get rid of them, and still do. The paperwork blizzard created by the checking-account system was so thick that a downhill slalom could have been held in the hall of financial institutions. More than four-fifths of the nation's economy was run through checking accounts, and some 90% of all payments were made by them. Handling those checks through the twenty operations from deposit to return was costing the banks, back then, anywhere from 13¢ to 25¢ each, was costing the banking industry billions of dollars every year. The number of checks in circulation increase at a rate of 7% compounded annually, which means the total doubles every ten years. There will be 41 billion checks to process by 1983, 160 billion by the year 2000! Today, some banks find that it costs closer to 45¢ to process a check. Multiply 45¢ times 41 billion to see what the banks face in 1983.

Point E is electronics. By handling all of this in-and-out on computers, those twenty separate operations could be reduced to one and the crushing costs of check handling could be drastically reduced. Economy-conscious bankers, data-processing people, even some governmental agencies like the Federal Reserve Board all agreed that one way to lead you willingly to electronicland and ultimately to Lifebank was to get you away from checks.

Early advertisements for the bank cards bellowed, "You can save time and trouble! Now! Buy all month long, pay for it with only one check!" By making lemonade out of lemons, the bankers were on their way to convincing you that they were the good guys doing you a favor. Down the road, they hoped that the billions of dollars invested in the credit card business would ease you into the wonderful, simple, profitable world of electronic banking. Coincidentally and conveniently, the same machinery could be used for both credit cards and for the planned Electronic Funds Transfer Systems, heart of Lifebank. Credit-authorization terminals, cash dispensers, automated tellers, automated clearinghouses, switching systems, data banks, and electronically tapped credit bureaus would all be needed for electronic banking, and were all needed for credit card operations.

The idea of credit cards issued by a bank wasn't too hard to sell. Many people were already walking around with one or more oil company cards, department store cards, airline, hotel, and restaurant cards. A high number of executives and businessmen were carrying one or more Carte Blanche, American Express, or Diners Club devices, cards basically designed for T&E (travel and entertainment) uses. When the two bank card systems were originated, both BankAmericard and Master Charge set out to get a piece of the spending being done on those T&E cards plus the oil company cards, travel cards, accommodations cards, and even some small retail cards. Although there was competition between them to get merchants to sign up and to get people to carry one particular card, they were joined in a common goal to establish a new kind of all-purpose credit card.

Bank cards were different. They added a heady third dimension to the types of cards in circulation. Until they appeared, cards fell into two categories: one-company and T&E. One-company cards are issued by oil companies, hotels, department stores, and other businesses like airlines and restaurants. There is generally no charge for these cards. The T&E's are a favorite with businessmen who do not want to carry a great deal of cash and who do need exact vouchers for company expense reports and for income-tax purposes. Usually, the T&E companies put no official limit on spending but charge an annual fee and closely monitor payment. There are unverifiable stories that charges as high as a half-million dollars have been made on these cards and that, once, a professional hockey player was purchased with one.

Although the American T&E cards (especially the bank-backed American Express Gold Card) are considered the most prestigious, they are all shoddy polyvinyl compared to one legendary French card. Back in the middle 1960's the House of Rothschild, most elegant of all French banks, announced that it too was issuing a bank card. The card would bear the emblem of that house plus the blue-and-yellow racing colors of Guy Edouard Alphonce de Rothschild, head of the bank. The card was restricted to use at only 120 of the world's costliest and most exclusive hotels, restaurants, couturiers, and stores. It could also be used instantly to buy a new Rolls Royce or Mercedes when the gasoline ran out on the old one.

Bank cards were not designed to be Rothschild cards. They were to be everyman's route to revolving bank credit, which was simply a short-term loan at high interest rates. These "all-purpose" cards were good for gasoline, hotels, restaurants, stores, just about everything. They were different from the T&E's because they did set limits on how much the individual could spend and the banks demanded that merchants get a clearance from an authorization center for purchases over a store's preset floor limit. With bank cards, extended payments were encouraged and, originally, the bank-rewarding interest rate in most states was 1½% a month, or 18% a year. These cards were not only free, but for a long while were forced upon people, and only in a few areas was there a onetime or annual charge for the card. That all drastically changed in early 1980 when President Carter's "credit-control" policies encouraged the banks to start levying annual fees or other charges for the cards.

They sat down and figured out the everyday advantages of the bank cards, the bankers did, and they sold them to you. Carrying a card was safer than carrying money, they said. You had itemized invoices for tax purposes. Shopping could be more efficient when you took advantage of sales when you were cash-poor, they promised you. Places which would not accept your check would accept your bank card, they assured you. And (ah!) all of your monthly purchases could be paid for with just one check, or better still, paid for with long, low, easy payments. The two biggest advantages were that bank cards were free and that they were available. Trying to avoid a free bank card during the first ten years of distribution was like trying to avoid the rain. The banks were off and running, running you into the great new electronic age of banking.

For people who sold goods or services, the cards were a mixed blessing. At first, bank card decals on the doors drew new customers and increased business, but a lot of it was fraudulent business and both the store and the bank lost money. After nearly every merchant had signed up for one of the two bank card systems, the advantage of belonging to one disappeared. The cards did give the small operator a chance to finance charge accounts, to service credit customers, and to keep money turning over because the banks paid up on sales slips immediately. The charge for all of this originally ranged from 2% to 7% of the amount spent by the customer, depending upon the store, its volume, and what kind of deal the retailer could work out. Those costs, of course, went right into added prices on what was sold, and you paid for it. The bank cashed in again—once in 12–18% interest on your financed account—and again on the kickback from the store.

With the airlines, railroads, hotels, restaurants, oil companies, and some 95% of all small retailers finally in the systems, the bank card chiefs set out to get the big stores also, to complete the total capture of all business. Only by having complete control of all retail outlets could a plan like Lifebank work.

It was not easy. The large operations like Sears, Penney's, Ward's, all have highly developed, efficient, and profitable charge operations of their own and needed bank cards with their kickback discounts like you need another payroll deduction. Sears, which is still the largest single charge operation and will remain so for years to come, felt that many customers bearing bank cards would be regular Sears customers anyway and that tradeoff could only weaken its own charge-customer profits. While Visa and Master Charge sales people continued to push for bank card acceptance at major retail stores, the stores said, "Who needs them?" In 1977, one of the years for heavy sales efforts by the bank cards, Sears had more of its own cards out than either Visa or Master Charge. The top three, Sears, Penney's, and Ward's, had more cards in circulation than both bank card systems combined.

The retailers had other problems with the bank card concept. Some were afraid that getting involved with the banks would be like inviting the lion to join the impala herd, that eventually the banks would devour them. Bankers, one said, think of themselves only as producers of money and wealth, while retailers work for the customers, who are the real producers of value. Another executive said that bank intrusion into retailing could bring violations of privacy in credit information, because both the retailer and the banks would have their own information systems and thus double the chances of privacy invasion. Still another was concerned that the banks would begin cutting out some of their customers, reducing the number to those the banks found most financially profitable. In some ways, he could already foresee the threat of a highly selective Lifebank system.

But the pressure continued. The bank cards were taking over the retail business even without the giants. The big stores began to see the handwriting on the sales slip. In 1978, credit cards put out by stores and other retail operations did 47.3 billion dollars' worth of charge business, but the bank cards were catching up fast. Their business was up to $44 billion and was only three percentage points behind on total United States credit card spending. At that rate of growth, bank cards would not just catch up, but would have 60% of the retail business by 1985, while the retail cards would slump to 25%.

J. C. Penney obviously looked at those figures and broke ranks first. It made plans to start accepting Visa cards in its stores during the fall of 1979. With that move, J. C. Penney became part of the unstoppable growth of Visa, part of the 3 million retail outlets which accepted Visa in over 130 countries. Sears also decided to "test" bank cards in selected areas to see how much new volume would be added to sales. Spencer Nilson, who publishes a widely-read, hard-hitting, bank card newsletter, estimated these cards would increase Sears' charge business from 11% to 14%. Ward's also joined in and decided to test bank card acceptance at certain stores. Some observers say that the retail giants have been "using" the bank card setups merely to strengthen their knowledge of credit systems. They will pull out of these arrangements when it appears they might be regulated like banks.

Dee Hock, the continually controversial head of Visa, came under bitter attack by some Visa bankers for the J. C. Penney deal. Instead of putting the Penney's transactions through a half-dozen banks so that they could make money, Hock and his board of directors agreed to sign Penney's directly with Visa. Visa people explained that Penney's joined with them purely for the technological advantages of the communications systems, and they had worked out a special low discount rate for that company. Penney's, already an outstanding leader in the credit business, with over 35 million cards out and $2.5 billion in annual sales on their cards, needed no lessons in conducting a successful credit operation. One observer commented, "Hell, Hock would have given them the services free to get the nation's second-largest stores—knowing that Ward's, Sears, and the other holdouts would have to be along soon." When J. C. Penney fell into line, Visa and the bank card business felt well on its way to the goal of complete retail control. Late in 1979, the Visa USA board changed that system's bylaws so any member organization could sign up major retailers.

One area in which the bank cards have not had too much

success is the food business. There have been continuing efforts to get shoppers to put supermarket bills on the cuff, but most didn't work. For example, Ralph's and Jewel, two large chains, both dropped their plans after testing them for short periods. Basic reason for the failure, according to one customer, "I just thought that food prices would have to go up if they took credit cards, and food was too expensive already." For supermarket operators, the amount of profit was small enough without being forced to give a kickback to the bank. One expert commented, "If bank cards get into a food market and encourage people who are short of cash to charge a steak they eat tonight and pay for next month, that is an irresponsible use of credit. . . . Once you are locked into buying food on credit, you can't get much lower."

But the bank card masterminds haven't given up. They are still working to get you to pay a finance charge and store operators to pay a discount fee on the average $6,000 a family of four now spends each year for groceries. In fact, right now the computer experts are figuring out ways to tie in the new supermarket automatic scanner checkout devices with the bank card electronic systems so you would get one food bill at the end of the month. From there, it is a slight sidestep to place your nutritional lifeline into your Lifebank.

Their plan moves on inexorably and thoroughly. There were, in mid-1980, 79 million residents of the United States brandishing over 125 million Visa and MasterCards. There were 164 million bank cards, worldwide. If you're average, you have some eight credit cards in your wallet, and two or three of them are bank cards. By 1985, if all goes according to plan, you could have seven or eight bank cards in your wallet, and fifteen to twenty of them in your family, or one all-inclusive "Lifebank Card." Today, the bank card people feel that they are close to saturation of the high-spending, high-financing type of domestic customer they want. Rather than go after the marginal people, the bank card people shifted their strategies. Until early 1980, the bankers had decided that the way to make more money was not with new people, but by getting you to spend more with more bank cards. That's why in 1978, 80% of the 20 million new cards distributed that year went to people who already had bank cards, to up their potential credit some $11 billion.

Another reality will be record profits for the banks. One speaker at a recent bank-card convention nodded to a couple of the men who are credited with pioneering the industry and said, "They have turned this business into solid gold." Even back in the tough days of the 1971 depression, when bank cards were still in their young-punk stage, the Bank of America alone is reported to have made 5 million pre-inflation dollars on its BankAmericard.

It got better. Visa's official and closely guarded figures show that the best three domestic banks doing over $60 million for the fall quarter of 1979 averaged 11.73% return on the bank card money outstanding and owed to them, and a high 14.32% finance rate on that money. After all direct expenses, which include salaries, data processing, advertising, furniture, entertainment, travel, even the money lost to bad credit and fraud, those same three high-performing banks showed $70.71 income for each thousand dollars card carriers spent on those cards. Even after the increasingly high cost banks had to pay for money, and an arbitrary internal "overhead" figure which bank management charges the card systems, those banks showed $32.00 net income per thousand. Based on $60 million income for that period, that lower figure still totals up to $1.9 million profit for those three months, or $7.6 million average annual profit for those "best" banks.

One Washington legislator whose main job is keeping track of the bank card business commented, "It's a gold mine . . . the credit card companies are mining this thing to death."

The profit picture was summed up by one banker who, in early 1979, said, "The card business is making more money for us than any other department in the bank, any other department."

By late 1979, however, that gold mine was beginning to peter out. The high cost of money was starting to cut into bank card income. As more and more money was removed from the lower-interest deposits and put into higher-paying investments, and as the prime rate increased, banks were forced to go outside for more funds and to pay more for them. More than

200 Visa USA programs showed that, on an average, they were paying over $4.50 more for each thousand dollars owed them. That increase popped up in the last quarter of 1979 when compared to the same period the year before. As a consequence, those banks also reported an average loss of $2.59 per thousand for the 1979 quarter, instead of the $2.55 profit they had averaged in the same quarter of 1978. There was no consistency throughout the Visa ranks. Some banks were squeezed but still made money, and others saw their card programs turn negative, both in profits and in bank management's attitudes.

As the cost of money swelled, there was moaning. Visa's Dee Hock said the industry barely broke even for the third quarter of 1979 and would show a loss for the fourth quarter. (His third-quarter reference was debatable, since an overview of Visa USA institutions showed net income of from $2.50 to $8.75 for each reporting bank's thousand dollars of volume, and no loss figures.)

Visa's Hock added that U.S. banks lost $70 million on card plans during the last quarter of 1979. The average loss was a little over $2.00 for each thousand dollars card users owed. He also predicted a $1 billion loss for banks during 1980. That statement made news but did not turn out to be accurate.

Hock went on the stump for a better bank break. "If the prime rate continues at its current level—and there are no signs it is going to go down—the situation will continue to get worse," he said. "Unless we see some action by state legislatures [to increase interest rates banks can charge on cards], some banks will have to seriously consider whether they want to continue offering this service to the public at all." Interest rates ranged, then, from 10% in Arkansas to 24% in South Dakota, with many stabilized at 18%.

Small and large banks reported trouble. The First People's Bank in Westmount, New Jersey, tried to sell its card activities to the Girard Bank in Philadelphia and, "They turned us down, and so did every other bank in the area," said that bank's chairman. New York's huge Citibank began to come up empty-handed, too. Several years ago, that institution had gone national with its ambitions and recruited cardholders from many areas outside of the Empire State. That program signed up a reported 5 million new customers, and those new customers along with the old were borrowing money at less than Citibank was paying for some of it.

But not all banks were on a profit diet. Chase Manhattan, United California Bank, Security Pacific Bank, Wells Fargo, Crocker, and others announced improved bank profits for the first quarter of 1980, despite the card industry's drain on their incomes. In fact, over 40% of the Visa banks showed a profit on cards.

Meanwhile, President Carter and his economic advisers sorted among odd possibilities to control inflation, which was running 18% nationally in late spring of 1980 and up to 25% in some areas of the country. To cut consumer spending, some experts advised activation of credit card restrictions. Under the Credit Control Act of 1969, Carter could pick out a credit area he wanted handled and then have the Federal Reserve Board set up new regulations to control it.

Not everyone agreed. Former Federal Reserve Board Chairman Arthur Burns and William Fellner of the American Enterprise Institute said that controls on credit cards would not be effective. Fellner also said they would be temporary and makeshift and the banks and consumers would find a way around them.

"It would be a symbolic gesture at best," added Otto Eckstein, president of Data Resources, Inc. "In terms of managing the economy, this is not where the problem lies."

"I think the administration is just desperately looking for something to announce, and one of the few things anyone can think of is to blame the bank cards," chimed in Paul A. Samuelson, a professor at MIT.

Even Paul Volcker, chairman of the Federal Reserve, agreed when he said the attack on credit cards "is a showy and symbolic one. We'll get some attention."

Credit cards were an obvious target. In 1979, card users spent $151 billion with credit cards. In mid-March of 1980 the Federal Reserve announced new credit restrictions. Included in the mixed bag was a fixed ceiling of 9% in credit-loan growth. To make sure the banks observed that limit, they would have to make a 15% noninterest-bearing deposit with the Fed for any credit they granted after March 14. The Federal Reserve knew that anything noninterest is definitely of noninterest to bankers.

At first, the banks were stunned. A no-growth policy in an industry which had set growth records? Restrictions on free (at 18%) enterprise? The end of the eternally elastic plastic?

But suddenly it was chocolate-chip cookies from home. Under the high-flying banner of doing their part to control runaway inflation, the banks could solve their financial problems overnight. Either just before or just after the credit-control announcement, the banks shrugged at existing traditions, regulations, or controls. Like good soldiers, they were "just following orders" to limit credit. Throughout the nation, the banks began to control your personal credit by charging you more for it.

Financial Notes from all over:

Bank of America, nation's largest, said it would begin charging cardholders a $12 annual membership fee, after earlier moves in which it increased the monthly payment and charged upward the way interest was figured.

Citibank, second largest, said it would issue no new cards, that card users would have to make higher monthly payments, and raised the kickback merchants have to pay them to belong to the system.

First National Bank of Illinois, ninth largest, announced a $20 annual fee plus larger monthly payments.

Crocker National Bank, twelfth largest, raised its annual 18% interest rate to 21%. In addition, it announced a 12¢ fee each time its card was used, even if the balance was paid off within thirty days.

Banc One of Columbus, Ohio, went to a $20 annual fee; so did Harris Trust of Chicago and First Security of Utah. Southeast Banks of Florida went to an $18 membership charge, banks in Denver and Seattle opted to settle for $12. Others began mixing and matching their options.

They were going every which way.

By raising interest rates, by charging an annual fee for the card, by charging merchants more, by adding transaction costs, and by introducing more profitable interest calculations, the banks were looking for the most profit with the least cost of existing business. Some, like Crocker, felt that charging an

30

annual fee would chase away an important number of card users. Others like Bank of America, felt that the fee was less scary than raising the interest rate and adding a transaction fee on top of that. Either way, after a short period of clutching, there were choruses of "Happy Days Are Here Again" ringing through the marbled hallways.

They looked at it this way: Bank of America had a reported 8-million-plus card customers who would have to pay the $12 annual fee or give up their cards. If one in ten decided to forgo the continuing pleasures of continuing debt, that would leave approximately 7.3 million customers at $12, or over $87 million annual income plus interest, breakage, and accelerated interest-figuring for that institution. Even if a very high 25% dropped out, annual fees would still run $72 million.

First National of Chicago's $20 fee for its 2.9 million card customers (minus, let's say, 10% dropouts) would come to over $50 million plus fringe benefits like interest earnings and other charges.

How about Crocker's 12¢-a-deal plus 21% interest? Figuring 900,000 customers who would stay with them at 12¢ a transaction for an estimated three transactions a month for twelve months, the take would be close to $4 million, plus the huge increase in interest income created by that bank's high 21% annual levy. Crocker officials felt that it would run much higher. They believed bank customers were more willing to pay a transaction fee and higher interest than the forbidding $10 to $20 annual fees being assessed by other banks. The ones with annual fees, of course, had finally caught up with the one out of three card users who pay their balance in time and contribute little or nothing to bank profits. The free bank card had gone the way of the free lunch.

Nowhere in the early announcements did the banks agree to modify or lessen the fees or interest rates when the prime rate went down, when banks could once again buy or attract cheaper money. However, they were forced to modify as the economic situation changed. Facing them was the problem of stiffer competition from other banks, especially at card-renewal time. Yes, individuals who wanted to keep one or more cards in mid-1980 would grudgingly pay the new tariffs, but what if a competing bank later came up with a lower annual charge or a less crippling interest fee? Card carriers would switch banks, take their accounts to the less expensive financial institution.

Suffering the most from cardholder attrition were issuers of cards that carriers considered "secondary" or backup devices. Faced with charges of up to $20 and/or higher interest rates and fees on each card, some bank customers began turning in the extraneous plastic. Visa holders suddenly decided they didn't need a second Visa or a third one plus one or more Master-Cards in their wallets.

While people were weeding out those unwanted bank cards, the banks were also using the credit crunch as an excuse to get rid of the chronic delinquents, the marginally profitables, the potential bad risks, along with turning down new applicants who were questionable assets to a solid, high-earnings card program. Quite a few banks also cut the credit limits for certain customers and on new accounts. In some cases, they did it for safety. But in many cases, those slashes gave them caches of unissued credit which could go to new applicants without violating the new regulations. Since those new controls said the banks were to use a base of already existing, already issued credit, the manipulators could take from one individual's credit-line surplus and dole it out to newcomers or even to more profitable, higher-spending card users.

Although the bank card public then had an ideal excuse to shred, cut up, or burn all of their bank cards, there was extreme reluctance to let go of the new money.

Bank cards have become so much a part of our life that in most parts of the country it takes at least one of them plus another credit card and driver's license to cash a check. Jails take them for bail, undertakers take them for coffins, cabs take them for fares, prostitutes take them for tricks, real-estate people take them for down payments, hospitals take them for surgery, dentists and jewelers take them for gold crowns, and thieves just take them.

In some cases, the bank card has become more valuable than cash: In Maryland, ten pornographic bookstores and a sauna outfit asked $3 million damages from Maryland National Bank in Baltimore because the bank wouldn't honor their Master Charge sales anymore. The bookstores complained that they expected to receive $1 million a year from credit card sales and that could be adversely affected if their inability to honor cards led to a "reflection on their reputation."

In other cases, bank cards were getting people into more trouble than just debt: In Beverly Hills, actress Louise Lasser, who played the lead in the television series *Mary Hartman, Mary Hartman,* tried to pay for a boutique purchase with an American Express card. The boutique accepted only bank cards. Ms. Lasser set up a row so upsetting that the police were called. Later, during a routine check at the stationhouse, newspapers reported that she had two outstanding traffic fines and was carrying a vial of cocaine. She had to post a $1,631 bail and face action ranging up to ten years in prison if convicted of drug possession.

In other cases, bankers tried to *look* different but stayed true to form. For Christmas 1979, the United California Bank ran huge ads encouraging people to cut down on their Christmas spending with bank cards. Officials of the bank, ordinarily busy encouraging people to expend their credit, said, "While we don't want to play Scrooge . . . it benefits no one when customers borrow more than they can comfortably repay." And one of their executives commented, "I've been involved with the pain of those who are over their heads in debt," and he assured everyone that the bank's "motives are straightforward—this is in our own enlightened self-interest, true, but its primary impulse is decent humanity for people in trouble." Other bankers chortled and slapped their knees, pointed out that with money costs way up and with an interest rate limited to 18%, UCB was merely trying to cool off bank card buying.

Like the bookstores, without a bank card our reputations could suffer; like Louise Lasser, if we kick up a fuss, the system will find other pressures in our lives to keep us in line; and like that UCB bank, the bankers will continue to insist that they are warm, loving, human, and concerned about us.

On the way from Point C (checks) to Point E (electronics), the bank cards have invaded, saturated, and altered our lives forever. They have become not a convenience but a necessity, not an innocent substitute for checks but a device upon which we will be totally dependent for financial and physical survival. On their way to the cashless, checkless society and more and better profits, the bankers have completely destroyed our long-standing American traditions of thrift, of saving, of self-dependence. The path to Lifebank is strewn with broken ideals, broken traditions, broken people:

There are millions of debt junkies created by the bank cards, ordinary good Americans brought up to believe in the good life but who received too much temptation too quickly, too easily.

There are tens of millions of homes in which both parents must work to keep up payments on their bank cards, leaving tens of millions of children to never experience a full family home life.

An estimated billion dollars is being stolen from the bank card industry every year by crooks, a billion dollars which you must pay. There are additional billions of dollars being invested in massive and complex electronic networks and systems for which you must pay. There are handsome salaries and fancy offices and expensive furniture and first-class travel and other luxuries for a whole new group of employees in banks and at Visa and MasterCard for which you must pay.

There is a growing and continuing loss of your privacy, as computers talk to each other, as unauthorized individuals gain entrance to your confidential files, as more and more bankers and credit bureaus and others poke into your life.

There is an increasing movement to depersonalize you, to make you into a number, which will simplify electronic sifting, sorting, categorizing, and handling of you.

There is increasing inflation, running at crippling rates, eroding your income and salary, destroying your savings, forcing millions to go broke or to exist in inhuman conditions. This inflation is heavily fueled and encouraged by unrestrained bank card spending. The credit controls were superficial remedies because existing bank cards had tens of billions of dollars of already approved credit which was not being spent. At the end of 1979, for example, close to 70% of bank-okayed credit for MasterCard carriers wasn't even being used. There is more than enough backup and reserve credit out there to double and even triple card-created inflation.

And, finally, there is the near-future threat of Lifebank, the system which will totally control us. It is not a someday utopia for the bankers but is already being built at some institutions in various parts of the country.

The bank card, today, is still the agent of debt, of spending addiction, of inflation, of loss of both privacy and freedom. Years ago, the B. F. Goodrich Company discovered that employees working with polyvinyl chloride could become fatally ill. One writer called it "an agent of death." That term might have been very appropriate: bank cards are made of polyvinyl chloride. With the threat of Lifebank, they could easily be the agent of death on a much larger, much more significant scale.

How did all of this happen from a little bank credit card experiment in California? Where did Visa and MasterCard come from and how did they take us over so completely? When did we weaken our sturdy American values and become robots for the moneymen? How did the computers gain control of our privacy and individuality? Where did our bitterly fought-for privacy go? Hasn't anybody been protecting us all along? Is there anything we can do about this, and if so, what?

Most of those questions can be answered easily, but some can't be answered at all.

2

E Pluribus Plastic

IN ONE RECENT year the government printed *$8–10 billion* in new cash; in buying power. It was not backed by gold, silver, oil, wheat, or anything of tangible value. Its only strength was the willingness of people to accept it, nothing more. By putting more unbacked money out there, the government diluted and cheapened the buying power already in circulation. Financial editors, professional economists, and business-college professors scowled once again, pointed a finger once again, and once again accused this irresponsible printing of unbacked money as the *major cause* of an inflation rate which approached 25% in some parts of this country.

Was it? Think about this:

In that same year, the bank card business distributed 20 million new cards which provided an additional *$11 billion* in buying power for most people who already had bank cards. Those cards also were not backed by gold, silver, oil, wheat, or anything of tangible value. Their only strength was the willingness of people to accept them, nothing more. By putting more unbacked credit out there, the banks diluted and cheapened the buying power already in circulation. Yet, despite the fact that those cards put a full 10% more spending capability into the economy than the government did, very few of those editors, economists, and professors blamed the banks as an even greater cause of the Incredible Shrinking Dollar.

The actual fact is that the modern-day, highly organized bank card industry is about ten years old. And so is our inflation. Although there are many contributing factors to inflation, such as the price of oil and the cost of housing, there is a noncoincidental and remarkable relationship between the growth of bank cards and the growth of inflation. The Consumer Price Index showed a 1.5% inflation rate in the years 1960–1966. There were a few local and regional bank cards— with which people spent about $86 million in 1967. From then to 1973, the inflation rate went up to 4.6%. This was the time when the bank card industry was becoming established, organized, and national. In 1973, $12.4 billion was spent on bank cards, an increase of 14,000% in five or six years! Wait, there's more. In the years 1973–1979 the consumer index inflation rate climbed to 8.6% and about $55 billion was spent on bank cards during the last year of that period; roughly, a 500% growth in bank card spending. Although the government's random printing of money and the costs of housing and oil certainly contributed to inflation, there is no doubt that giving people $55 billion a year in additional and unbacked buying power has helped to shove the inflation rate skyward. Later figures showed both the inflation rate and bank card spending still clambering upward.

United States Representative Frank Annunzio from Illinois said, "Before bank cards, when you wanted to borrow money from a bank, a trained loan officer decided whether you were sound enough for the loan, responsible enough to pay it back, that the loan was for a good purpose, and that you weren't going over your head into debt. Today, consumers are being given several bank cards, all with high credit limits, and they are the loan officers, deciding where it goes and how much to spend. Since many people are using this money to buy today because prices will just be higher tomorrow, you can bet the inflation rate will not only stay as high as it is but will keep growing."

He added, "A good 20% of inflation is due to credit cards, through direct and indirect effects. We can cut government spending but not consumer spending. How deep is the credit card habit? Did you notice that during the gasoline shortages that the stations which took cards had lines twice as long as those which didn't? Deficit spending can cause as much damage to the family as it does to the federal government, probably more. We have figures which prove that most bankruptcies are caused by credit cards."

One of his aides compared us all to the alcoholic who received an unsolicited bank card and put it on permanent deposit at his local liquor store. He drank himself into insanity. It is his opinion that we have put our unsolicited bank cards on permanent deposit with the merchants and are spending insanely.

An economics writer said, "The soaring rate of inflation, which averaged over 13% last year [1979] . . . would have increased more than 10% *even in the absence of oil-price hikes.*"

Bankers tend to scoff at the accusation and continue to point to the swollen price of oil as the prime reason for our inflation.

In late 1979 a banker from the MasterCard system spoke at a bank card convention and asked, "Are bank cards helping to fuel inflation? We hear continually that people have never before relied so much on borrowed money to maintain their standard of living as inflation erodes their disposable income. Consumers are freely borrowing to buy durable goods in order to avoid paying higher prices later on. Americans currently owe $21 billion on their Visa and Master Charge cards, but more importantly, they have—by some estimates—more than $40 billion of unused credit. In fact, it has been estimated that the total credit card purchasing power in this country exceeds $262 billion. Is it not at least possible that the use of our cards to beat tomorrow's higher prices is at least an inflation sustainer?"

The year before that, newsletter publisher Spencer Nilson had also brought this situation to the bankers' attention. In one of his 1978 publications he said that credit card carriers who were then spending $43 billion on bank cards had an additional $219 billion they could spend on all cards if they wanted to. He also pointed out that anybody could print and issue plastic money so that federal control over the currency it printed meant very little. He felt that the real spending power was in plastic cards and that the bankers should get control over how they could and could not be used.

Visa's president, Dee Hock, didn't agree with all of this pointing-with-alarm. He criticized the criticizers, insisted that the bank-card carrier is very smart. "People don't suddenly get dumb because we give them a piece of plastic," he was fond of saying. To prove his point, Hock used the example of two neighbors who own houses. Ten years ago, one borrowed money on his house to invest in additional real estate. The other played it more conservatively, didn't remortgage, continued to pay off his home. Today, Hock made his point, the man who borrowed money on his house is paying off the loan with cheaper dollars and has undoubtedly made money on his other investments. The man who just sat by and paid off his house is watching the money invested in that house get cheaper and cheaper. Hock's stand was in defense of more bank card borrowing to buy more durable goods and to pay off later in cheaper dollars. It is that very thinking which strengthens our inflation.

Also defending bank card spending was Robert M. Duvall, vice-president in charge of consumer lending for the Bank of New York. In an interview he said, "It's the old economic wheel. We simply won't be able to keep production rates up and keep unemployment down if we didn't keep that wheel going, economists tell us." His belief was that the old-fashioned way of saving up until we could afford a car, a television, or a stereo set for cash just didn't move the economic wheel fast enough.

But another banker didn't agree with him and warned, "Even if cardholders don't use all of their available credit, don't overborrow, there is still the danger they will overspend. When people run out of money in their wallet or watch their checkbook balance get lower, they tend to stop spending. With credit cards they just keep on going. The fact they're not using everything the banks have given them is just proof that the banks have given them way too much."

A university economics professor said, "At work, surrounded by research and statistics, I think the bank cards are not adding that much to inflation. But when I see how the cards are used at my house, I change my mind."

Bankers, like economists, obviously do not agree about inflation in particular and economics in general. Economics is a very complex subject. Listen to the top moneymen. They do not agree with each other about how money or value works and how it should be handled or controlled. If they had the answers, we would not have depressions and inflations.

You do not have to be a professional economist to understand how bank cards can create and sustain inflation. You do not need a doctorate in economics to understand the history of money, the gradual removal of money from its backing by gold and other security devices, the effect of foreign currencies on our own economy, or even how our complex Federal Reserve System works.

All you have to understand is that money is purely a simple, convenient medium of exchange. Originally, coastal-dwelling natives traded fish and decorative seashells to residents of the interior for hides and brightly colored stones. Later, in a more agrarian society, farmers traded grain for meat, or fruit for tools. However, transporting tons of wheat to the village to exchange for yard goods, a plow, and a horse was awkward and impractical. Direct barter was replaced by easy-to-carry symbols like precious metal, minted coins, gems, which had a value of their own. But the problems of loss or theft or even bulk and weight called for even more portable and safer indications of value. Paper currency, IOU's, bonds, letters of credit, checks, and other lightweight devices became the better way to exchange value. At first, these symbols were backed by equivalent value in precious metal or other security. But gradually they took on their own value, based upon trust in the companies, or financial institutions, or governments which issued them. They all became a form of credit, a belief in the value of the symbol and what is behind it.

So the bank card is also a form of money. Like other symbols, it is a medium of exchange.

Even the government accepts the bank cards as a form of payment, or cash. In early 1980, for the first time, the Government Printing Office agreed to accept Visa or Master Charge cards in payment for a book. That book was the 636-page basic U.S. Budget book. Ironically, the price of the book was raised from $4.25 to $5.00 because of inflation.

Three important changes happened in this century, changes

that demanded that money be redefined, redesigned, almost reinvented.

First, people began to move around more during the early 1900's. The automobile, the streetcar, and the railroad gave people the ability to go across town or across the country in reasonable times. If there was employment available in the next town, it didn't take a day's ride by horse to get there. People moved to be closer to employment, to loved ones, to the increasingly attractive bright lights of the expanding cities, leaving rural life behind.

Next, the industrial age created an organized factory system which scheduled paydays. At first these paydays were once a month or, at best, once every two weeks. That was a long time between income, and many families ran out of buying ability before the next pay envelope was due. Smart operators of groceries, dry-goods stores, and clothing emporiums realized that, and began advancing credit to their regular customers "until payday."

Then, information systems appeared. Data processing went from crude punch cards to bulky computers, then to the finely tuned microelectronics systems which could handle millions of bits of information and transmit or receive them over long distances.

These revolutions in transportation, communication, and retailing created both problems and solutions. The new mobility of people meant that they were strangers in new settings. The hometown merchant who knew them and was glad to carry them until payday was left behind; in his place now was a suspicious new clerk who didn't know who they were or whether they were good for credit. There was what Dee Hock called "a crisis in identity." The clerk was forced to telephone the bank or the factory to find out if the stranger actually had money and a job. Eventually, computers took over that task and the credit or bank card became both a symbol of identification and a promise to pay. A miner from Pennsylvania was no longer a stranger in Virginia. A farmer from Iowa could be recognized as okay in California.

Actually a form of credit card can be traced all the way back to the Middle Ages, when Central European knights avoided carrying money because of bands of thieves who would ambush and rob them. Instead, they wore specially engraved rings which were used to stamp the bill at an inn. Later, the innkeeper could present that bill to the knight's home castle for payment.

The bank card began to replace money for buying things. For the stores, it was good identification of the buyer and guaranteed payment from the bank. For the customer, it was safer than carrying cash, identified him to the store, and allowed him to borrow against next payday or even against twenty paydays ahead.

Along with currency and checks, the plastic bank card had become money. It didn't look like money, but it spent like it. Credit cards changed our standards of living at home, changed the way stores did business, changed our economy, and contributed substantially to our inflation.

These days, the government economists are giving us a lot of pig latin about what causes inflation. There are many theories. With most of them, smoke is being blown into your face. Inflation is very simple. Look it up. Inflation is nothing more or less than an increase in the amount of money that's in circulation compared to the amount of goods and services that are available. The more money around, the more people will spend. The more they spend, the higher prices become. The higher the prices, the more spending power people want or need, and the more they get, the more prices will increase. That's why we have a wage/price spiral. That's inflation in action.

The bank card helps to create inflation in two ways. First, the cards allowed $55 billion to be spent on credit during 1979; $55 billion of money other than cash and checks, which was added to the economy. Two-thirds of that created money was being borrowed and financed and was not offset by immediate cash payment. Second, with over a total of $260 billion available for spending on all cards, everyone could become a big spender. People were no longer limited to what cash they had, what checks they could write.

The government began to erode the dollar, first by reducing the precious metal which secured it, then by removing all precious-metal backing, and finally printing money as though it was a throwaway shopping news. That new money was to cover governmental obligations for defense, for health and welfare, for education, for foreign aid, for the creation of jobs, and for other government programs. The new money, piled on top of the amount already in circulation, drove prices up and the value of the dollar down. The post-World War II dollar will buy 25¢ worth today. There was a lot of hueing and crying about this by economists, and the media picked it up. People began realizing that their money was shrinking and/or prices were growing. It suddenly made good sense to spend now before prices went higher. Yesterday's $4,000 Chevy was suddenly $8,000. Ground beef was priced like yesterday's sirloin. A decent turntable cost what an entire stereo set used to.

That was the logic, but there was also the emotion. It also felt good to spend, to give up those self-sacrificing days of "should"-and-"ought" scrimping. Any nagging doubts or left-over guilts were easily handled because "it made sense" to buy now and save, pay off with cheaper dollars down the road. Besides, there was suddenly a lot of money around to spend. Some bus drivers were making $25,000 a year, some factory workers were raking in $35,000. That was the kind of income traditionally associated with doctors and lawyers (who were now up to hundreds of thousands a year). Instead of comparing that income to new prices, the bus drivers remembered how much that used to be and began spending as though it still was. The rich once spent $8,000 for a car, so spending that amount for a car meant you were rich. A while ago, you could buy four nice small homes for $100,000. Today, in urban areas, it may buy one. But owning a $100,000 home does give a lift to the ego. Especially since that house will probably be worth $125,000 next year.

With inflated income and salaries and with the additional buying power given to them by bank cards, people began feeling that they were getting ahead. They were wrong. The system is not balanced. The inflation rate has been growing much faster than income increases. The discouraging fact is that income has been going up only about half as fast as the cost of living. New wages and salaries have gone up about 7%, while prices have risen about 14%. A new round of raises and more spending would encourage the inflation rate to go even higher.

The banks, of course, make out like robber barons during an inflation. They know that you are losing money every minute, growing poorer by the month. They know that a very large percentage of bank card users are spending that credit money just to stay even, just to continue surviving. They know that most can't pay off those debts immediately. That debt will be financed at very rewarding interest rates and/or with fees and charges, all profitable.

Things are even better elsewhere.

Although not a bank card, the American Express Company admitted that inflation was good for that company. Chairman James D. Robinson III told the Los Angeles *Times*, "Our average spending will be four times that of the bank cards. . . . Our card members are higher spenders." He added that he was concerned about inflation, but that people will take vacations (remember the psychology of enjoy now, pay with cheaper dollars later). Vacations are no longer an option, but have become a staple in our lives. Because of this, American Express continues to make record profits every year.

The way things are going, you will be able to spend even more. Recently, the average bank-card family had about $3,700 available in credit on five cards. That's just the basic Visa and MasterCards issued to them by different banks. More credit is coming. More bank cards are coming. Although technically these new cards will not be "bank" cards because they are not basically issued by a bank, they are bank card-type. They work like a bank card, are used like a bank card, are handled like a bank card. Other organizations, called "affinity groups," are being given permission to issue bank cards, just like the banks. Today, Visa comes not only from banks but also from car-rental companies, savings-and-loan associations, chain stores, the American Automobile Association, and others. Visa officials have been under attack by many of their member banks for allowing nonbanks into the system. But this path does encourage the Visa system to grow, does push Visa into a continuingly stronger role in the bank card industry, and can possibly hold off some antitrust, antibank action which a large but ignored outside organization might file against that card.

Someday, you may get a Visa card from your American Legion post, League of Women Voters chapter, Corvette Club, Italian-American Society, YMCA, and alumni association. After that, it is possible that your supermarkets, department stores, automobile dealers, hotels, and restaurants will be asking you to take theirs. The circle will have caught its tail. There will be a wide assortment of Visas (and MasterCards), each issued by one organization, but good everywhere. You'll have a pocketful of plastic again, all controlled by the two bank-card groups. Each organization will be pushing, prodding, pressuring you to use its particular card. You will be given a possible total of $10, $15, $20 thousand to go out and pollute the inflation rate even more. In fact, bank card historian Nilson says the bank card spending possibilities could be one-half trillion dollars by 1985!

What will be the effect of all this credit or new money? Today, in some areas, one out of every 25 families files for bankruptcy. In 1970–1971, the average BankAmericard user who financed his card purchases spent $16 each time the card was used, and owed the system $229 in a given month. Eight years later, in late 1979, the same group spent an average of $34.34 each time the card was used, and owed "the banks" $461. The bankers say that's not so bad, that the growth is about equal with inflation. What they are looking at are percentages and averages. The fact is that not everyone owes $461. Some owe $25. Some owe thousands. The people who owe thousands are the ones in deep trouble. They are in hock for months or years ahead.

Economist Alan Greenspan said, "A fifth of all households owe no debt at all, so the percentage of income going to debt service [paying off what's owed] is close to a third. A significant number of households must be allocating nearly half their incomes to debt service." Not only that, but if you have a take-home of $300 a week and payments on your debts are taking half of that, you're probably going to have to use your bank card more, borrow even more, just to survive.

Trying to keep up with inflation is like betting into a full house with a pair of deuces. And using the money the bankers are lending you to do it is a way to go broke even faster, because you're adding high interest to the already crippling national inflation rate. If you can afford to lose that kind of money and still survive, tell the government people. They would like your secret.

But the government is better off than you are. History, that information from which we never seem to learn, proves that whenever a country suffers runaway inflation, it eventually goes bankrupt and has to destroy its worthless money and come up with a new form of value. With that new money, those countries rebuild and eventually are strong again. Germany, for one, went bankrupt after World War I, but today its deutschemark is one of the most stable currencies in the world. You can't do that. Bankruptcy wipes out everything you own except the few survival items they let you keep. *You* can't go to a different value by printing new money at home. *You* can't change the ground rules the way countries can. *You* have to live with the way things are. And the way things are, you will not only lose everything in case of bankruptcy, but may never recover from it.

Balancing out what bank cards have done for and against us, one legislator said, "Let's get rid of them. We lived without bank cards for 180 years, can't we live without them now?"

Another idea going around Washington suggests, "We need a Regulation W like we had during the Korean War. That required 25% down on any major purchase, to keep inflation down and to keep people out of debt. We need it more now than then. Hell, the banks only ask a small monthly payment on what people owe. And then their bill goes up at a high interest rate when they do that. No wonder we have such debt and such inflation."

A more organized plan for controlling bank cards might include (1) limiting each person to one Visa and one MasterCard, (2) putting a sensible and practical spending limit on those cards, (3) reducing the profit potential for the banks, instead of increasing it as was done in the spring of 1980.

Chances are, none of these controls will happen. Bank cards or the financial devices which will replace them will be as much part of your future as the national debt. They are too profitable for the powerful financial structure, too supported by the retail

46

establishment, too easy and painless for people not to use them.

A form of Regulation W could be introduced to Congress, but its chances of passing would be small. Even if it was voted into law, the final draft would be diluted and ineffectual because of bank lobbyists. The resulting law wouldn't solve the problem.

Limiting each person to one card from Visa and one from MasterCard would only hasten the day when one card will be like ten, when your assets will all be collected in that impending Lifebank against which you can draw in different ways. It is a step which would help the bankers, not you. Putting a limit on your spending with those cards could also be easily violated by the Lifebank system. With Lifebank (if the bankers could be prevented from controlling that account, which won't happen) you could get credit against your cash savings, against your life-insurance equity, against your home mortgage, against other assets, and have multiple credit lines to get you into trouble.

Trying to reduce the profit motivation for banks is like trying to stop a mad grizzly with a BB gun. Card profit-control laws could be passed, but then the banks would sock you with a collection of membership, handling, carrying, processing, and billing charges to get around them. Bankers are not part of the public-welfare system. Profit is what bankers are about. As far back as 1971, Visa's Dee Hock was worried about bankers' greed. He claimed in a speech that greed had caused many bank card problems.

Is there anything practical that can be done? Yes. We'll get to that simple solution later, after we've taken a solid look at how this financial trap was intricately designed, carefully assembled, and electronically hooked up to take over and control our money and how we use it.

Your bank card is just as much money as the cash in your wallet. The old advertising campaign which encouraged you to "Think of it as money" eased you into that realization.

Dee Hock admitted this, has said, "Visa is a currency card with a credit feature." In other words, borrowed money that could also borrow money. Even though the Federal Reserve Board is the only organization legally permitted to manufacture money, the banks have overtaken and even passed it in turning out buying power.

"Banks have been engaged in the indiscriminate issuance of credit," one expert suddenly realized. "It's the same as issuing money . . . and should be carefully examined."

He finally caught on. It's time the rest of us did.

3

Time to Cash Out?

Hoping for a little leniency, the Chicago mugger looked up at the judge and said, "Your Honor, you got to look at it this way. Me 'n' the banks are in the same business. We both take money out of other people's pockets. Only difference is, I'm more direct about it."

Telling that story at a recent credit-card-convention cocktail party, the narrator ended with, "You know, that's another excellent advantage of the credit card—it gets rid of money, of cash, and that gets rid of a lot of crime."

Does it? Let's see.

Cash, of course, attracts crime.

In San Francisco, entire busloads of passengers are systematically robbed of their cash and valuables by roving gangs of teenagers.

In Chicago, one strongarm gang leader explained that they had taken to daylight attacks "because there are too many muggers out there at night."

In St. Louis, a representative of a cabdrivers' group reported, "Cabs used to be something that took you, now it's us that gets taken."

In New York, a bank manager complained, "We not only get

held up for cash in the banks, but our employees get held up on the way to and from work."

It's the same everywhere. Everywhere there's cash. Each year our local, state, and federal law-enforcement authorities release official crime figures, always boiling explosively upward.

Assault on citizens (mugging) up 55% in most areas, armed robbery of businesses up 65%, burglary up 76%, each year, every year, read all about it in your local *Tribune*. And each year these figures accelerate at a rate which makes the inflationary spiral look like a broken pinwheel. Nine out of every ten crimes involve burglary, assault, mugging, larceny, theft, or robbery. They are all aimed at supplying the criminal with either hard cash or property which can be easily sold on the street ("Hey, mister, want a good deal on a watch?") or fenced through underworld sources. And more than nine out of ten of these crimes are committed in our major cities, home of over 170 million of our citizens.

Cash. Without it, would these once-strange, now-common signs of the times be needed?

"Repair truck only. No cash."

"Exact fare only."

"Driver carries no more than $5.00 in change."

"Credit cards only after 6:00 P.M."

"Bank deposits made hourly. Only $25.00 in cash register."

"This safe is open and empty."

And one enterprising bank card executive even came up with the suggestion a few years ago that the bank distribute a large celluloid pin to each credit-card holder. That pin, to be worn on the lapel of people on the street, said, "I carry no cash." As the banker said, "It's not only a great promotion for credit cards, but we'd be doing a public service, protecting people from muggers."

Since cash has no personal identity, is relatively untraceable, is accepted just about everywhere for just about everything, and since inflation has caused most people to walk around with more of it in their pockets, cash is the easiest and best target for criminals.

Cash *could* be considered the biggest *cause* of crime. It is the single most dangerous threat to our personal and collective security, the most debilitating demand on our police departments, and the major basis of a national traumatic fear of our own streets, neighborhoods, and cities.

As one mayor of a major city said, "I thought when I took the job I was going to be a municipal administrator, not a general in charge of neighborhood warfare."

Nor is the crime-creating aspect of cash limited to dirty little muggings, crippling old ladies for their purses, shooting kindly candy-store operators, or burglarizing someone's loved home. At the higher levels, criminals play for higher stakes, but it's still all, or mostly, cash.

There are questionable figures around, but no one truly knows how many businesses and industries are owned, how many political offices have been bought, and how much our lives are controlled and managed by cash purchases made by organized crime. Much of that cash comes from the estimated $2.3 billion a year people "drop" gambling at legal locations like Las Vegas, and the additional billions people spend betting with the bookies on the outside. Other important cash comes to organized crime through prostitution, numbers rackets, blackmail, extortion, kidnapping, payoffs, and the biggest seven of them all, narcotics.

No one knows how much cash is being misered away in secret foreign bank accounts and vaults by individuals who make killings in cash and who sneer at paying their fair share of local, state, and federal income and other taxes, leaving others, like you, to pay more than a fair share.

No one knows how much cash is being embezzled every day by corporate officials in heavy industry, by motion-picture producers, by chain-store accountants, and by bankers, thereby robbing their organizations and their stockholders of honest income.

No one knows how much cash is being used every day to bribe senators and representatives, governors and mayors, judges and juries, city councilmen and county supervisors, patrolmen and deputy sheriffs, into turning highly dangerous or insane criminals back onto our streets or into passing and enforcing laws which benefit special-interest groups by stealing from the rest of us.

And no one knows how much cash is being traded and

exchanged to support and strengthen the already catastrophic narcotics trade in this nation. From the "nickel" bag of marijuana sold to schoolkids on the playground to the $100,000 leather pouch of cocaine delivered by chauffeured limousine to the motion-picture producer's Bel Air home, it's a cash-and-carry business.

Only cash makes these crimes against us possible.

Money is still thought of as cash. That's the way we were trained. "Cash in hand." "Cash on the barrelhead." "In God we trust, all others pay cash." These phrases were drummed into us as part of the American Way, along with "Fourscore and seven years ago . . .", "We, the people of the United States . . .", and the Notre Dame fight song.

Cash is, to us, money. And money is addictive. The more people seem to have, the more they seem to want or need. Stockholders demand hefty annual increases in dividends. Laborers insist upon sizable wage increases. Welfare recipients petition for more. Even beggars insist upon the sound of crinkle instead of the clang of coins these days. Throughout the nation, churches, charities, public utilities, insurance companies, colleges, hospitals, and politicians fight or weep for more cash, more money, for their work, their institutions, and themselves.

To supply this demand, to keep everybody happy, and to continue the legend of ever-spectacular American economic growth, our government mints and prints cash. There was a time, and not so long ago, when paper money was backed by precious metals. Money could be redeemed for gold, and later, silver. It said so right on the currency. Today, newly printed money is not backed by gold or oil or lumber or steel or cattle or shares in AT&T. It is backed only by trust, it says so right on the currency: "This note is legal tender for all debts, public and private." You have to take the government's word for its worth.

When the government prints new unbacked money, that money borrows from the future, which is also what credit does. That new money is a major contributor to our inflation. With more money decreasing the value of each existing dollar, the government programs, stockholders, laborers, colleges, public utilities, hospitals, etc., want (need) more, so more money is printed, on and on in an increasingly uncontrollable circle of events.

Some economists say that this nonvalue-backed money and the inflation it has helped create is one of the greatest dangers the United States has ever faced. The people look to Congress for help. Congress looks to the president. The president looks to the Federal Reserve Board, and that group of financial wizards tries to head off higher incomes and higher spending by jacking up the discount and rediscount rates which banks pay for money, forcing banks and other lending institutions to charge more for loans, and by putting "controls" on credit. The federal officials and Congress try to help by increasing or decreasing taxes, increasing or decreasing federal spending. Since this federal spending is generally deficit spending, money we're all borrowing from tomorrow, you probably feel it's okay to do that too. That's where the credit card comes in. After all, if the government can spend over its head, why can't you? The logic is sound. With that logic, then, some 600 million credit cards are put out there in the marketplace to buy up what's available, at any price, since inflation will only cause it to cost more tomorrow.

Yet, every day, grim-faced so-called experts try to balance out such volatile areas as unemployment, personal-debt delinquencies, housing starts, and gross national product to see if they can find a four or even a five in these days when two and two make six.

Today, even cash, in the form of trust, is a major contributor to all of this. That trust has even replaced gold as the backing for cash. Today, gold is sold for cash or for a form of credit based on cash. The person who sells that valuable gold sells it for trust. He trusts that the currency or credit he accepts for that precious metal will be of *value*.

Look at the value devices in detail.

What about cash as a form of value? It has problems. Cash can be lost, destroyed, stolen. It's bulky, hard to handle, wears out, is confusing, doesn't carry the same value in different parts of the world. It also costs money to print, mint, replace, circulate, protect.

Checks? Checks are another form of value. But checks are

awkward to handle, have to be individually prepared, can be easily destroyed or lost or hiked or forged or counterfeited. Checks have so many problems that most places of business demand a driver's license and two credit cards as identification before cashing or accepting one these days. In addition, checks cost the banks somewhere between 25¢ and 45¢ each to process, and the resultant multibillion-dollar expense for check handling is passed on to you.

And then there's credit. Credit is a form of value. This form of value (not necessarily the credit card or rating of the person holding credit) cannot be destroyed, lost, altered, forged, counterfeited, stolen. It is not bulky, does not wear out, does supply a complete record of any and all transactions, and gives the consumer leverage in disputes with merchants who sell him shoddy goods or bad services.

Credit is completely portable. Credit provides total availability of your money twenty-four hours a day anyplace in the world, or will, when the systems are in place very soon.

Credit gets rid of cash-based crime.

Businesses and industries can't be bought with credit cards. "Hi, there, fella, would you take my Visa for your dry-cleaning store?"

Secret cash caches aren't possible or practical with credit cards. "I'm sending my MasterCard by courier for deposit in your vaults."

Tax evasion is difficult with credit. "Yes, Mr. Howard, I know you say you made only $14,000 last year, but you spent $75,000."

Embezzlement becomes a comedy routine with credit. "Let's see, I'll just remove this $50,000 from the company vault and make a double entry of my credit card."

Bribing is difficult with credit. "I was thinking, Senator, if you could find your way clear to vote for that li'l ol' dam, you might find a plastic gift in your office tomorrow."

Gambling is extremely limited on credit. Ask any gambler. "Five grand worth of chips on your name? Only if your name is Secretary of the Treasury."

And, finally, coke on credit, marijuana on MasterCard, Midnight Express on American Express? If you believe that, you've had too much of one of them. For the narcotics trade to survive, it must depend upon the difficult-to-trace and anonymous form of cash between grower and processor, processor and shipper, shipper and distributor, distributor and dealer, dealer and buyer. Any form of traceable paperwork, any type of recallable computer input, could threaten the entire chain. Besides, credit is based upon trust, and as one dealer reported, "Putting trust in a junkie is like putting a pop in him. It's fantasytime."

In addition, credit, personal credit, gives you the same advantages companies and corporations have had for years, financial backing to smooth out the high and low economic periods of your life.

Because of the disadvantages of cash and checks and the booming popularity of credit and credit cards, some bankers are whistling a nonmelodic tune called "The Cashless Society." That is the scheme in which all of us would be controlled by an international system of value and value exchange. To moneymen, this system has the inherent advantages of allowing governments and financial groups to increase, decrease, and change the value of your value to keep the nations and the world on a balanced economic scale. To you, the cashless society would mean no more checks, no more cash (except for a few coins), and a lifelong membership in the International Fraternal Order of Debtors.

Your fraternity card would be your credit card or cards, and just about everything you do today with cash and checks would be done with those plastic rectangles. (By then, it could be another device, like a Little Orphan Annie decoder pin or some such, but so far, nothing has replaced the card.) That credit device would be the combination credit-access symbol and the identification tool you would use to pay your rent or mortgage, outfit your home, buy and repair your car, travel on vacation, take you out to dinner, pay for the insurance, the kids' educations, the hospital, attorney, dentist, your clothing, haircuts, shoe repair, manicures, togs, frocks, just about every purchasable item or service. Even small purchases like newspapers, cab rides, bridge tolls, will probably be sold in coupon books, by extended subscription, or with coins bought with your credit device. And as Visa's Dee Hock projected, payment will be automatic, painless, and electronic. You read details of that frightening futuristic program in Chapter 1.

That cashless society and your own personal Visa (or Master-Card) to it almost sounds too good to be true. Is credit too good to be true? It is.

It is, because there are frightening and dangerous problems with the cashless society and the credit card life.

First of all, it would be possible for you to lose all of your "cash value" (formerly cash savings and checking-account balances), because even with credit controls, the banks have overextended themselves in giving out too many credit cards, allowing too many credit-card holders too much credit. *The Nilson Report*, a credit card newsletter, said that there will be 255 million bank credit cards in this nation by 1985. There were approximately 125 million at the end of 1979. Although the credit controls put a slowing effect on issuance of new cards, no one expected that clampdown to last too long. The *Nilson Report* went on to say that some $2.7 billion will go to charge-offs by 1985. Charge-offs are bad debts, credit-card bills that aren't paid by the people who use the cards. That staggering amount of bad debt could easily result in some bank closings, and it's common knowledge that the governmental agency that insures your bank accounts could not handle a major run on several large banks at the same time.

Second, privacy may be something you get in your home but nowhere else. Credit files in the cashless society would (and already do) contain complete dossiers on your employment, your income from all sources, and your spending habits. By running computer analyses of your expenditures, investigators can easily find out what you buy and how you live. The report will undoubtedly also contain complete records of your social and political affiliations, marital history, antisocial behavior or criminal record, military or governmental service, and personal habits including dope, alcohol, sexual preferences, and more. Every piece of information you've ever entered on a question-naire in school, at the doctor's, at an employment office, on a voter-registration form, anywhere, will be automatically in-cluded, along with additional data dug out by credit reporters. All of that information on you will be available to bankers, credit people, and (although bankers say no) governmental agencies and others. More about this later.

Third, you will be forced to pay for all hidden costs involved in the credit card industry. You will pay for the complex international maze of computers, the huge and high salaried staffs of the credit card administrators and employees hired by that industry. You will pay, directly or indirectly, for the card, the imprinters, the processing system, the data banks, credit investigations, the discount the merchant pays to be a member of the credit card system, and even for the invoice you receive telling you to pay. These hidden costs can add up to important expenses for you. For the first quarter of 1979, a Visa study showed that salaries, employee benefits, advertising, furniture, space, and other overhead added up to an average of $43.94 for every one thousand dollars of sales. The merchants paid in $18.47 for every one thousand dollars in sales, money the merchants recover by charging you more for goods and services. And the cost of funds, the money the bank must pay to borrow money to lend to your credit account, averaged $36.09 for every one thousand dollars in volume. All of that money for overhead and for the cost of funds is not borne, good-naturedly, by the bank, but is passed on to you. You pay for other hidden charges, too. You pay for those bad-debt write-offs, for those multimillion-dollar fraud losses, and even for arbitrarily set "overhead" charges each bank passes on to its card operation. In rebuttal, bankers point out that cash costs money to print and circulate and to protect and that checks cost money and that the costs of the card system are less.

Next, you will become a victim of the electronic age; of unreasoning, unthinking, unheeding computers. Computers not only make errors but also insist upon repeating those errors until they are reprogrammed. Since reprogramming is a time-consuming and expensive task, computer personnel tend to delay it. Nearly every credit card holder has a horror story about a computer error. Some credit card holders have been brutalized by these computer errors, which ended up costing them huge amounts of money for attorney's fees, and for paying off incorrect purchases and mounting interest fees. It has cost some people even more—loss of their good credit reputation—all because of computer error.

In addition, you will be living in a society which discourages thrift, encourages free spending. With an estimated 700 million buying devices in circulation by 1985, with credit spending becoming the accepted life-style, you will be expected to go along with it, to do your part for the economy, the nation, and the banks. If you don't, it could mean major problems in obtaining not only the luxuries but also the necessities of life. If you do, you could end up in continuing debt the rest of your life. Benjamin Franklin's homilies about thrift will be replaced by then with a quote from Artemus Ward, "Let us all be happy and live within our means even if we have to borrow the money to do it with."

And finally, should you lose your job, become ill, have a bad year with investments, or diminish your income in any way, you could become a discard. Discards are people for whom the cashless society has no use, so it discards them by dis-carding them. When you lose that credit card and your credit standing, you will literally not be able to survive. With no cash, no checks, and no credit, how can you? By begging? By growing your own food? Perhaps. But probably not. Today, there are already an estimated 16 million discards, people who cannot qualify for a credit card or who have lost theirs through nonpayment of bills. Today, even with checks and cash still operational, these people have great difficulty getting into hotels, renting cars, cashing checks, even shopping in certain stores. By cashless-society time, when checks and cash are obsolete, the discard may find death preferable to loss of credit.

So, there's the choice:

Cash. It's bulky, awkward to handle, wears out, is backed with nothing of real value, is expensive to manufacture and to protect, can be too easily printed, which leads to financial chaos, and it is the cause of 90% of all crime in this country.

Checks. They are easy to forge or counterfeit, hard to cash, must be individually made out for every transaction, backed by nothing of real value, cost the bankers billions a year to process, which is passed on to you.

Credit. It can bring about bank failures and even overall economic failure, loss of privacy, expensive hidden costs and interest rates, computer error, reduction of humans to ciphers, overspending as a way of life, creation of a group of discards, economic undesirables who may not be able to survive in a credit economy.

Billions of dollars are being spent annually to take you rapidly and inexorably into Dee Hock's value-exchange cashless society. The computer-system designers are ordering bigger and better communications equipment to track, monitor, control you and your money. The stores and the merchants are pushing you into more and more card buying, fewer cash or check sales. The marketing and advertising men are busy coming up with campaigns promising you a better, fuller, more enriched life with slogans like "It's better than money" and "We're keeping up with you," as though you had asked for this and they were merely being accommodating.

There is one aim, one desire.

Many bankers want us to check out of checking, and cash out of cash, and put everything into a Lifebank.

But before we make that decision, perhaps we should know more about how this money monster was born and how it grew.

4

Dealing the First Cards

OBSERVED THE RETAILER trying to peer through the blossoms of credit card stickers obscuring his front door, "To think that twenty years ago there was no such thing as a credit card."

As a matter of established fact, that storekeeper was off by some sixty years. Credit extended to customers who were identified by cards or plates has been with us through most of this century.

Back in the very early 1900's, several hotels encouraged good feeling and continued patronage from steady customers by offering them cards good for occupancy and some hotel services. Even the most science-fiction-oriented hotel executive of the time probably never dreamed of the day when that idea would enable nearly everyone to buy nearly everything nearly everywhere. From a place to lay one's weary head, the credit card today can be used to take sky-diving lessons, pay the rent, back a crap-table bet, learn the bassoon, board the cats, get out of jail, ride a ski lift, get buried, ride a cab, rent a person-of-the-evening, invest in stocks, support the church, ride a roller coaster, fill a house and all of its closets with furniture and furnishings, have an operation, support a political candidate, and if so inclined, even take a 38-stop trip around the world with walking-around cash so minimal it wouldn't bulge a leotard.

By the beginning of World War I, some large department stores were issuing dogtag-looking metal plates to favorite customers, but the war slowed down the credit movement. It was to be the first of three setbacks for credit cards because of wartime credit restrictions. By the early 1920's, when Johnny was home and working again, credit cards were being distributed once more. By 1924, the Tin Lizzie could be filled up with one of those newly introduced gasoline-station credit cards. Easy credit grew and spread during the middle and late 1920's. From the "pay-at-the-end-of-the-month" corner grocery stores, credit even invaded the conservative stock exchanges, allowing many customers to overload on stocks bought on low margins. Some of that marginal credit is blamed for the crash.

Interest in single-use credit cards (good only at one place) went down as badly as the market when the crash came. They were replaced with cash-down layaway plans, installment buying, and "money only" at hotels and filling stations. By the late 1930's, though, when defense plants were rolling up to three shifts a day and the economy was reviving, so did some credit cards. But not for long. World War II restrictions severely limited credit spending, and the cards and plates became souvenirs, like "Win with Willkie" buttons.

Most economic historians credit the birth of the modern plastic multiuse (good-in-many-places) credit card to a man named Frank X. McNamara. Operator of a small loan company, McNamara noticed that one of his customers, who had a large number of department-store charge accounts, would lend out his charge plates to friends and charge for use of them. He paid the outstanding debts with loans from McNamara, pocketed the difference between interest paid and interest charged. However, one of his "customers" finally became tardy with payments or vanished, and his enterprise collapsed.

Stuck with some outstanding debt, McNamara was discussing recovery possibilities at lunch one day with his attorney, when he had an "aha!" His inspired idea was based on developing one charge plate or card which could be used at many establishments. Since the idea came up at lunch,

McNamara decided that the ideal group of businesses for such a device might be restaurants. McNamara put up $25,000 and the attorney, Ralph Schneider, $15,000. Additional money was raised from other intrigued investors.

In February 1950 the modern credit-card industry was born out of a three-room suite in Manhattan's Empire State Building. Going into business, the fledgling company had a list of twenty-two signed-up restaurants and one hotel, all in New York. Named Diners Club, the business lost over $58,000 in its first year. However, in its second year of operation, Diners Club did over $6 million worth of volume and made a profit of over $60,000 after taxes.

That same year, 1951, New York's Franklin National Bank developed a sales-credit plan for stores which bankers consider the great-granddaddy of bank credit cards. Since Diners was purely a travel-and-entertainment card, Franklin's program was the first multipurpose retail card. Meanwhile, in California, the huge Bank of America was perfecting plans for a bank credit card, plans which had been in development since 1946.

In the late 1950's and early 1960's, a small odd lot of banks began issuing credit cards on a local basis to their most creditworthy customers. Included were such giants of the industry as Citizens & Southern National Bank in Atlanta, Marine Midland Trust Co. of western New York, Mellon National Bank & Trust Co. of Pittsburgh. The highly conservative Chase Manhattan Bank of New York went into, out of, and back into the credit card business, all between 1959 and 1969.

In 1958, the American Express organization, watching the growth in Diners Club, became hungry for some of those profits, went into the travel-and-entertainment-card business itself. Carte Blanche was to come later.

By 1963, some 200 banks (out of a national total of 14,000) had jumped into the credit card field.

After a while, for many, everything looked black except the ink. Even though the Bank of America was operating in the heavily populated and wealthy state of California, losses on its credit-card program, estimated to be upward of $8 million in the late 1950's, became frightening. Other banks also took a nonliquidity bath. By late 1963, of the 200 banks which had gone into credit cards, only 75 were still running programs.

Meanwhile, what most bankers didn't know was that the Bank of America had crossed over from credit card losses to profits in the early 1960's. This fact was kept quiet. One executive of that bank admitted, ". . . unaware of our relatively quick crossover to profitability, [other banks] left us alone in the credit card vineyard . . . I must admit that whenever they showed interest, we became expert in that noble art of 'poormouthing.'"

"Bankers are the world's worst businessmen," one Washington official commented. "Can you think of any other business which has to be protected from competition by law?"

It may be that because bankers are bad businessmen, some of the first ventures into the credit card business were such fiascos. Initial expense for setting up programs was inordinately costly. New and expensive equipment, new personnel, new communications systems were all necessary for such programs. Banks, which are not noted for giving away anything, were allocating heavy overhead and rents to the new credit card programs, putting them under crushing debt before they had issued card one. Although these costs were a matter of internal paperwork, nearly every department of a bank is expected to be self-supporting and to show a profit. For the newborn credit card operations, the baby was stuck with hospital, doctor, and swaddling expenses.

More importantly, some programs couldn't survive because of an unworkable circle. In order to get people to carry and use cards, it was essential to get merchants to accept those cards. And in order to get merchants to sign up, the bank had to produce impressive lists of cardholders. While chasing this tail, the credit card executives were also stuck with very expensive advertising and marketing programs designed to sell the credit card concept to the world.

By 1965, bankers throughout the country had finally caught on to Bank of America's poormouth act, had found out that it was making excellent money with its BankAmericard. Turning mottos to the wall which said "Once stung, twice shy," profit-hungry bankers began trekking to the money mecca—Bank of

America headquarters in San Francisco. BankAmericard personnel did share information about operations with many of them, and as the numbers of seekers increased, so did adroit shuffling of appointments so that rivals from the same city or area might not encounter each other in the halls.

As banks in various cities began start-up operations for credit cards, intense competitions developed which were followed by advertising wars, special promotional offers, and even sabotage of each other's systems. In one case, Western Pennsylvania National Bank (now known as Equibank) issued a card called Cash-Master, which was actually just a check-cashing card which could be used in stores and supermarkets throughout the greater Pittsburgh area. Officials at another bank, Mellon, realized that Cash-Master could easily be converted into a credit card. Credit card experts at the time were convinced that it was essential to introduce the first credit card in a community in order to be successful. Mellon also heard that another rival, Pittsburgh National, was planning a credit card and made a resolution to get its card out first.

Pittsburgh National moved into the credit card arena by purchasing a local credit card company. Mellon went to the Bank of America, and its people were slicked into buying an outdated computer program which Bank of America was just discarding. As one official who was around then noted, ". . . we created our own mistakes at Mellon, while PNB bought theirs."

For ordinarily slow-moving bankers, it was suddenly a fast track.

Mellon's first visit to Bank of America was on August 9, 1965. By October 13 of that year, the Melon credit card people had made a recommendation and a presentation to top management to go into the card business, received approval, bought the B of A computer program, put together a list of 200,000 customers who met the bank's credit standards, mailed out cards, signed up three thousand merchants, hired and equipped and trained one hundred people in credit card operations, and put together an extensive marketing and advertising program—all in sixty-six days!

In setting up their program, PNB tried to buy ten thousand

imprinters (the in-store machines which transfer information from a credit card to a sales slip) but found that Mellon had bought up the full inventory from the only two companies which manufactured them. PNB was almost out of the card business before it was in it, but an extraordinary and enterprising executive named Charles Russell (later one of the top men at Visa) came up with a day- and face-saving solution. Why not just encourage the merchants to use the Mellon machine until Pittsburgh National could supply its own? he reasoned. Round two to Russell.

Faced with that answer, Mellon officials fretted and fumed, finally went to the manufacturers of the imprinters and said, "We want you to put a small pin in the bed of the imprinter that will stick up higher than the credit card by one-quarter inch." Since these companies were also making the credit cards which would be used in those imprinters, Mellon officials ordered a small spot cut out on the edge of the Mellon card which would fit around that pin. The end result of this imprinter incursion was that when Pittsburgh National cards were used in the imprinter, they either broke or were badly bent and couldn't print a sales slip. Merchants began turning down PNB's cards. Round three, Mellon.

Some merchants fought back by tearing out the pins, but finally PNB delivered machines of their own to settle the dispute.

End of encounter, probably a draw.

By 1966, credit card fever had infected bankers across the nation, and that epidemic nearly killed the card business.

The worst sickness showed up in Chicago. There, First National with its "First" card, Continental Bank with its "Town and Country" card, Harris with its "Charge-It" card, plus Central National and The Pullman Group, were all in a frenzy to be first, and dumped a conservatively estimated 5 million unasked-for credit cards into the mails. Professional unemployables, dogs and cats, infants, the dead, were all sent credit cards in the mail. Some homes received four, five, six, seven cards. One young lady, not wanting to use them and not quite understanding how the system worked, gave the seven she received to friends, told them to go out and have a good time.

Mail thieves, suddenly realizing that an unsigned card was equal to a full wallet, took to ransacking mailboxes or robbing mailmen and then selling the cards on the open market or illegally using them.

Faced with this sudden gift of *mañana* (I'll pay tomorrow) from the mails, if not from heaven, hundreds of thousands bustled into stores, bought up everything in sight. At one toy store near the affluent North Shore, credit card-equipped purchasers waited in line over an hour to check out counterloads of Christmas gifts for the kids.

Mammoth piles of bills came pouring into the banks from the merchants. One bank's files were so overflowing, extra bills were kept in cigar boxes. The merchants wanted to be paid immediately, as promised, and not to pay rapidly was to lose the merchant and to endanger the entire system. So the banks paid, but the card users didn't. New credit card users considered the monthly bill one that went underneath the doctor's and the dentist's and the other bills that take fourth or fifth priority in bill paying.

In addition, fraud became business-as-usual. Found to be using fraudulent cards were mailmen, boardinghouse or apartment dwellers who "just happened" to find a stray card floating around on the lobby mail table, janitors and garbage men who suddenly discovered cards which had been thrown away, and the professional thieves and gangs which bought cards at street prices, then went through unsuspecting stores with a scorched-shelves policy. One estimate says that during the height of the illegal card use, some 10% of all cards "put on the air" (mailed out) were misused or illegally used. One gang, which included retail-store people, gas-station operators, and a post-office employee, plus others, ran wild for two and a half years in that area and did five banks out of millions of dollars. The FBI refused to issue any estimate of fraud from their files, but the Post Office Department admitted that card fraud went up 900% from 1966 to 1971.

The banks were responsible for losses not only from the criminals but also from the law-abiding, nonpaying customer as well. In their hurry to be first with a credit card in the market, banks had not been too careful in selecting their mailing lists.

Some were from bank files, but others were lists of supposedly creditworthy people which had been purchased from outside services.

A later study, conducted for the Charge Account Bankers Association, showed that only one-fifth of all banks investigated had checked the backgrounds of people who received cards by mail. One out of three banks used mailing lists of people with whom the bank had no direct experience.

Nor was this lack of judgment restricted to Chicago. When the United California Bank put their card "on the air" in 1967, only minimal financial responsibility was demanded. Individuals who had a minimum monthly balance of $150 in their checking account for two years were considered good prospects for cards, and received them.

The Californians were much better about their mail drop. Only a few trusted employees knew the mailing dates. But the next year, when cards were to be replaced, the credit crooks were ready. Knowing that the banks would have to replace the cards at about the same time, mailbags and mailboxes were pilfered, many cards stolen. One batch of fifty stolen cards cost the Wells Fargo bank $200,000, and that bank's fraud charges for 1968 came to $780,000, which was a crippling 1½% of volume.

Meanwhile, while one department of the bank was trying to recover outstanding debts, other departments were continuing to mail out new cards and encouraging their use through promotional stunts, through free incentives, and through advertising campaigns. One Chicago card, called "Town and Country" ("It has a nice classy ring to it," said the man who indicated that his wife had thought it up), was losing so much money it was getting a bad name. "Let's change it," said one bright copywriter at that bank's advertising agency. "It's getting everyone, including the bank, in debt so fast we could call it Supercharger!"

Overall, because of the careless list buying, the nonprotected mailings, lost cards, fraud, slow repayment, the Chicago "drop" is considered the major disaster in the history of bank credit cards. Those operations are still referred to as an example of greed and bad judgment whenever bankers get together.

The basic problem with bank cards of the period was that use of the card was limited to an area served by the bank. In California, which has branch banking, the card could be used statewide but still was just so much worthless plastic in Arizona, Nevada, or New York. In Chicago, which does not have branch banking, the card was good only in that city and not even downstate. Finally, a group of the Illinois banks got together and organized a cooperative called the Midwest Bank Card. Under that plan, a central organization was set up for handling sales slips made by any member's card. They designed a basic card format, made plans to handle administrative details, and even planned a regional hot-card list which merchants could use to detect stolen or lost cards.

So card acceptance went from a local to a highly limited regional use, but what was needed, bankers and card carriers agreed, was a nationwide system in which a card could be used anywhere.

On March 25, 1966, Kenneth Larkin, later executive vice-president of Bank of America, gave a memorandum to the managing committee of that bank. Larkin proposed that Bank-Americard be developed nationwide by licensing certain banks to use the name, the format, the program, and the systems. Two months later, that bank began the push to make Bank-Americard the national bank card.

At about the same time, four other large California banks decided that they were not interested in promoting rival B of A by issuing its card, but would start their own. The Bank of California, Crocker-Citizens National Bank, United California Bank, and Wells Fargo founded an association which was designed to compete with Bank of America both in California and, eventually, nationally. It was called the California Bankcard Association, and many other California banks hurried to sign up with it, to get in on California's greatest gold rush since Sutter's Mill. Banks in Idaho, Nevada, Oregon, Washington, Utah, and Wyoming also came in, and to acknowledge them, the name was later changed to Western States Bankcard Association. July 1967 was its start-up date.

When an idea's time has come, it comes all over. In January 1967 a group of banks from Pittsburgh and from Virginia,

Washington, and other states set up an organization called the Interbank Card Association to develop something called the Interbank Card. Attending that meeting was a member of the California Bankcard Association who was there to get permission to use the words "The Interbank Card" on the card being issued by his group and to set up a loose national affiliation. The name of that California card was to become "Master Charge" (although that name had not been originated in California, had actually been obtained by the California group from the First National Bank of Louisville, which had inherited it through a small company it had bought).

Before developing one national look and one national name, member banks of the Interbank system were all issuing their own cards with their own looks and their own identifications. The only cohesive device which held the cards together was a small "i" in the corner of the card, indicating membership in Interbank. Watching the growth and success of Bank-Americard, which had the same name and the same look everywhere, Interbank finally obtained the rights to use the name Master Charge from the California group and the single-look white card with overlapping red and yellow circles was adopted by other banks in the system through the next several years.

The Interbank movement was greatly strengthened when the Eastern States Bankcard Association was formed and supported by New York's gigantic Chemical, Manufacturers Hanover Trust, and Marine Midland banks. Their decision to offer the new Master Charge card would open up the highly profitable New York market to all Master Charge cardholders from elsewhere in the country, and would make Master Charge a true coast-to-coast, or national, credit card.

By January 1968 the Interbank group said that it had 6 million cardholders and 150,000 merchants. It was a good start. But BankAmericard was setting ambitious goals for it. The blue-white-gold card was accepted in forty-two states and seven foreign countries, had 16.7 million cardholders and nearly 400,000 merchants by year's end, through B of A and its licensed banks.

Choosing up sides became the game bankers played. First

National City Bank (now known as Citibank), third largest bank in the United States then, was faced with the two growing systems and finally decided to abandon its already established 1.3-million-member "Everything" card and go with Interbank and Master Charge. Three other major New York banks and other founders of the Eastern States Bankcard Association also decided to give up whatever cards they were issuing at the time and go to Master Charge.

The basic difference between the two systems was that BankAmericard was a monarchy and Interbank was a democracy. The Bank of America, staunch in its belief that one tightly run and highly organized system was best for all, forced licensed banks to operate under demanding rules, regulations, and fee structures. Interbank, however, was a group of loosely related associations, run by committees. For getting things done, for putting together a highly efficient and workable system, BankAmericard was best, operated like a West Point close-order drill squad. For freedom from stifling regulations, for permitting each bank to set its own general credit card policies and procedures, and for giving each bank its head, the Interbank group was best. Today, although there have been major changes made in both systems, especially at the blue-white-gold one, the same comparisons are still made between the two.

Some of the banks which had joined the BankAmericard system found that certain enforced regulations didn't work well for them. They also resented what they considered to be prohibitive fees and charges. Others had so advanced and professional a credit card operation, building on the B of A's initial instruction, that they were outstripping that bank in technology, procedures, and even profit performance. Their petitions for changes were met with little cooperation at Bank of America. "B of A is as flexible as a vault door," said one banker.

Unsuccessful at getting what they wanted, some important banks and blocs of smaller ones made threatening sounds about leaving the BankAmericard family and, just possibly, joining up with Interbank. Faced with that, the prospect of losing business, possible antitrust action, and finding the difficulties of administering the licensing program almost unbearable, Bank of America officials gave in.

In July 1970 an organization called National BankAmericard Incorporated was put together as an independent, nonstock membership group owned by its members, in proportion to their sales volume. In other words, Bank of America owned a lot more of it than, let's say, a small bank in Iowa, and, therefore, had a lot more to say about how things would run. In fact, the Bank of America had five members on the board of directors the first year, compared to only one director from each of seventeen other banking firms who were on the board. The agreement called for that number to be diminished by one member each year for the first four years, leaving B of A with one member on the board from the fifth year on. There were also financial arrangements agreed upon with Bank of America, payments to be made during those early years. All of the banks in the nation which were licensed to the BankAmericard system canceled those licenses and became charter members of NBI.

A slight bespectacled banker from the Northwestern part of the United States, with the uncannily apt name of Hock, Dee Hock, was elected president of the newly formed group. Hock suddenly found himself in a very expensive chair and a very hot seat. He had to soothe, calm, mediate, and settle the long-standing, sometimes bitter feuds between B of A and some of the member banks. It was, on the surface, a no-win situation for him and would require the wisdom of the Chinese philosophers, the Greek tutors, and the Renaissance essayists to handle this situation. Fortunately, Hock was an avid reader, was familiar with the advice and methods of everyone from Confucius to Socrates, from de Sade to Thoreau, and used them all in handling headstrong bankers, truculent employees, temperamental suppliers. Some observers noted that the mixture sometimes ran two cups of de Sade and a teaspoon of Edgar Guest.

By this time, credit cards had bypassed the novelty stage, were as permanently established in most wallets as a driver's license. With nationwide credit now available, a person could get rid of all those single-use cards in the wallet, reduce paperwork, and pay monthly bills with a single check, discontinue carrying large amounts of losable and stealable cash, take advantage of the built-in credit card financial records, and even help himself to a small loan, a cash advance, through the mighty bank credit card.

Playing "catch-up" very rapidly, the Master Charge groups had put together thirteen computer centers to handle the interchange of sales slips. The largest and most sophisticated center was located on Long Island and handled details for 220 banks in the East, Midwest, and South. These "smart" machines not only sorted out who owed what to whom but also alerted security officials if a card was being used in a suspicious manner, say, for purchase of three television sets in one day or five wristwatches.

Despite "Nixon's Depression," as the period was called, BankAmericards were used to spend over $2.7 billion in the United States during 1970. That was roughly 60% more than had been spent with those cards in 1969, yet card demand and distribution came to an almost complete stop because of the economic climate. That meant people with cards were spending more with them, less with cash and checks—the beginning of the bankers' dream.

Part of that growth in spending was traceable to the banks' increasing role as pitchmen for the cards.

Economic evangelism was the keynote at the 1969 annual conference of the Charge Account Bankers Association.

In one speech delivered at that meeting, the speaker said, "To generate the major sources of income, cardholders must use their cards more and more often, from more and more merchants, for more and more purposes and for larger and larger amounts and on more and more extended terms . . . it will be necessary in many cases for you to help teach the consumer new shopping habits and give up old ones— especially if the bulk of her purchases must be shifted from present retail establishments to those . . . members of your plan . . ."

Chalk-striped, tie-pinned, crew-cut bankers began shilling for the bank credit card, like late-night TV pitchmen pushing genuine emeralds for five dollars.

Some banks began offering small incentives for any use of the card; theater tickets, small electrical appliances, even minor cash rebates were offered as rewards for initial card usage.

Other banks began offering blank "credit" checks which could be used to pay taxes, purchase goods, or in some way get the credit-wary to begin borrowing money.

Still others were sending out special mailers, promoting credit card use through telephone solicitors, and developing psychologically tested advertising campaigns which soothed, calmed, and reassured that debt was the American Way of Life and thrift went out with either Ben Franklin or his stoves. "Think of it as money," said one campaign. "It's nicer than money," said another. "Why don't we just say, 'It's better than money'?" one bank advertising manager asked his agency. "It is, for us and also for them."

Out west, the Bank of America, and others, began dreaming up publicity stunts to get the card promoted in newspaper stories and on human-interest television shows. Most of these activities centered around the survival of an individual in a certain location or locations for a given period of time armed with only a bank credit card and perhaps a few dollars in change for minor purchases.

One bank in Ohio persuaded the residents of a Columbus suburb to join in a six-month experiment to see if the credit card could replace cash and checks. About 20,000 special cards were mailed out by City National Bank and Trust, and of that number, 8,000 were used in the highly publicized experiment.

One observer commented, "When people first got the card, they swore they wouldn't use it, but this experiment encouraged usage on what appeared to be a limited and protected basis. After first use, when the bills came in, most paid right away to avoid finance charges. That went on for a while, but pretty soon, purchasing habit on the cards increased, as did the balances, and finally, interest fees became a way of life."

Another enterprising group discovered that the "limit" put on an individual's spending with a card was being misused as a cutoff point and instead should be used as a transition to get people to spend *more*. At first, individuals approaching their limit of credit were warned not to exceed it. However, after the new spending-psychology plan was approved, those same people were merely contacted (by telephone in the store or by mail at home) and asked if they wouldn't like to have a higher limit, more money to spend on credit. A study showed that some 90% of the people given a new higher limit would then spend somewhere between the old limit and the new one. Today, of course, with most card families having two or three or five different bank cards, limits run into multithousands of dollars. When buyers reach the limit of one card, even in the middle of a transaction, they merely reach into the wallet and pile plastic until the purchase price is reached.

But all that glittered was not gold everywhere. Because of the unexpectedly high cost of going into the credit card business, because of inexperienced and sloppy management, because of unmanageable fraud losses and slow payment during the 1970–1971 period, some banks were being forced out of the card business.

According to the Federal Reserve Board, $115.5 million was lost on credit cards in 1970. That was more than 50% higher than the losses suffered by the banks the year before.

The Riggs National Bank, Washington, lost over $1 million for the year through its credit-card operation, blaming it on "unusual fraud losses, high credit losses, and nonrecurring expenses due to operational problems," according to that year's annual report.

The Bank of the Southwest, Houston, also lost "slightly in excess of $1 million," but its annual report was more philosophical, chalked it up to "another part of the maturing process of the credit card program."

In other cities, where losses were estimated to run into multimillions, banks refused to tell how much money had been lost. However, Aetna Life & Casualty Company, which had developed insurance to protect banks against stolen or lost or counterfeited cards, reported that losses were so high as to be "absolutely fatal" to some banks.

One spokesman for that company said that a major contributing cause to these losses was dishonest merchants. He told how a small luggage shop had 117 fraudulent sales in one month, and how a drugstore had sold $42 worth of bubble gum to one customer but couldn't recall that unusual sale. He accused the banks' reactions to this thievery as being "notoriously slow or nonexistent in some cases."

Larger banks were also losing money handling credit card transactions for the smaller banks that worked through them. In order to cut losses, one bank, the $11-billion-deposit Manufacturers Hanover Trust Co., New York, actually cut off the thirty-six smaller banks it had brought into the Master Charge business, leaving them with no overall workable system for their credit card programs.

Nor was money the only loss. The bankers also lost some business freedom on October 26, 1970, when President Nixon signed Public Law 91-508. That broad bill, which had been cut and pasted together from three other pieces of legislation, covered such diverse areas as tax evasion, secret foreign bank accounts, and stock frauds. The credit card industry was also singled out for regulations and controls. Under the new law, banks were forbidden to put their cards "on the air," to send them to people who hadn't asked for them or who had previously turned them down. Too, the liability of a cardholder was limited to $50 per card if that card was stolen, lost, or in some way used fraudulently and without the cardholder's okay. Lobbyists for the banks took the edge out of total protection, however, by encouraging inclusion of complex conditions which allowed many exceptions to the rules. Neither bankers nor consumer protectionists were totally happy with the law. The bankers promised to continue fighting it, while the consumerists also pledged to keep fighting, but for additional card and credit control.

By the end of 1970, the bank card industry resembled a high-stakes poker game. That year's pot of $6.1 billion in consumer spending on bank cards was in the middle of the table, the credit card operations with weak hands had dropped out, and BankAmericard and Master Charge were set to raise their bets to an eventual showdown. Both systems were about even. Each card was then represented by over 3,000 banks, each claimed more than 20 million holders, and figures showed that about half of them were actively using their cards. Master Charge was good in forty-nine states, BankAmericard in forty-four, and the others were being signed up fast.

What had emerged was the traditional and legendary American two-rivals system. Like Republicans and Democrats, like Union and Management, like Pepsi and Coke, BankAmericard and Master Charge had control of the bank card business, had transformed the idea for a dining-out chit into a much-wanted new form of personal identification and money for a high percentage of Americans.

With the increasingly profitable money coming in from the merchant discounts or kickbacks and with the high interest on unpaid balances being paid by nearly two-thirds of America's 40 million bank card holders in 1970, BankAmericard and Master Charge began to go for each other's throats, to get deeper and deeper into our pockets.

5

Playing Showdown to a Pair

"Now, we're really going to get into Hock," scrawled one member of the bank executive officers meeting on a note he passed to another. The receiver, the story goes, observed the notation, added one of his own, and sent it back. "No man is a profit in his own country," it said.

Coming out of the humor closet, where bankers are seldom found, those two execs were not actually very punny. They were in reality stating the bank card industry-wide conflict which revolved about Dee Hock, the man chosen to head up the newly formed National BankAmericard Incorporated staff command headquarters, flying its blue-white-gold banner.

Hock, who was to help lead the nation into his name, was speaking at an NBI Chief Executive Officers' meeting in New York in early 1971, delivering alternate passages of pep talk, morality play, philosophy lecture, and tactical maneuverings concerned with BankAmericard's upcoming thrust for leadership.

The card bankers throughout the system were getting to know Dee Hock a little, and their initial reaction was love, hate, or perplexity. Some days they were fiscally comfortable with the slight, conservatively dressed banker from Seattle who had been chosen to lead their card crusade. When he talked about debits and sales volume and delinquencies outstanding, they nodded in the boardroom sunlight and murmured appreciatively. At other times, he might show up in that clothing style known as Tinfoil Baroque and lecture endlessly on what the banking industry could learn from Aristotle, Confucius, and Emerson.

To a large percentage of the bankers, these references were identifiable only as the first names of waiters at Greek, Chinese, and British restaurants. What this group did not want was an orator; it wanted a heavy-handed, hardheaded, solidly grounded financial genius who would show them how to cut their bloodying losses and how to conduct and profit from their card programs.

Hock gave a fig. He was dedicated to giving them things to think about as well as things to do. He believed that many bankers had absolutely no idea of the enormity or potential of the bank card and their overall responsibilities in keeping that product and service from self-destructing.

That early 1971 meeting gave the bankers a good look at the Sermons on the Mount-ing problems they were to hear from then on. Hock declared that he was a firm believer in the natural order and inevitability of credit as the modern form of exchange.

One of his favorite comparisons was with the old crossroads country store where the farmer "borrowed" the seed and tools to plant crops in the spring and then paid the storeowner what was owed at harvesttime in the fall. The modern-day bank card was the current version of that old tradition. Sort of plastic on the barrelhead.

His most fervid pronouncements were about the individual's "crisis in identity" these days. The bank card was not, he preached, the greedy banker's device for driving people into debt, but a sorely needed service which told a merchant that a buyer was good for the money, even if he had a face straight from a post-office wall. In that respect, then, the card was really not a credit card at all, but actually a "currency" card that had a built-in borrowing bonus.

From Hock's masthead in 1971, the bank card was but a tiny atoll, and he was looking for continents. At year's end the year before, the average BankAmericard customer used that card to purchase about $30 worth of goods a month and, if financed, paid interest of $3.60 a month. Hock scoffed at those figures by saying that the bank card's penetration of the market was insignificant and that the potential was unlimited.

However, in confidential remarks, he also warned the bankers against greed. "Like dogs in a yard full of chicken bones, if they chew carefully over an extended period they wax fat and happy. If greed gets the better part of them and they bolt sharp bones, they may die of a perforated intestine. While it may not prove fatal, there are some perforated intestines in the bank card business," he lectured.

Then he added, "Must we grow 100% a year? What is wrong with 25% compounded annually if it is consistent with quality, adequate control, and reasonable expense?"

A lot of the audience didn't want to hear that. They wanted the Big Casino right now. The problem was losses. In the sixty-four working days of 1970's fourth quarter, people with BankAmericards had spent an average of close to $13 million a day. But, of that amount, some $313,000 a day went down the drain as fraud or bad debt. Some of the banks were hard hit. One terrifying example to the other bankers was a member bank which was running 22.6% delinquency ratio compared to its gross sales. There were others running 16%, 15%, 13%. A delinquency is a cardholder's failure to pay the minimum amount due thirty days after the free period is over, or roughly sixty days after the bill came in.

Not all banks were in trouble. Some of those with superior management had cut their delinquencies as low as 1.3% and 1.4%. But even those banks were giving their card programs the once-over and the card bankers a good going-over.

The American Banker, newspaper of the banking business, said in the spring of 1971, "It is a time of mounting problems—a time in which fraud and credit losses are soaring; when restrictive legislation is on the increase, and when processing costs have climbed far beyond expectations.

"Among the large banks, at least a few in metropolitan areas have run up such heavy losses that they are almost ready to give it all up and get out of credit cards."

The basic problem was that when a bank lends money it has to get that money somewhere. It either comes out of working capital or is borrowed from someplace else. The reason banks stay in business and make money is because they use their money profitably every day. If outstanding money has also been borrowed, then the loss can be twice as high. For example, if a bank has $25 million out in delayed payments and that money had been invested elsewhere instead at a steady 10%, that would be at least $2.5 million a year the bank isn't earning but could be.

Some banks were so hard hit by slow payment and losses that they almost got out of home mortgages completely, out of construction loans, out of retail and international divisions. Many laid off employees, cut back on executive salaries, slashed internal budgets, advertising programs, bonuses, and expansion plans.

Other banks began outright restrictions on who could qualify for a card. Anthony Burgess, the distinguished British teacher and author (*A Clockwork Orange*), tried to get a card in Texas and was turned down even though many of his low-income students had wallets stuffed with Master Charge, Bank-Americard, Diners, Carte Blanche, and American Express. At the other end of the country, however, a dog in Michigan received an unasked-for credit card application.

There was a highly critical period in 1971. If some of the banks hadn't started making money, bank cards would probably have been melted down into Tupperware, the initials NBI would have reverted to the National Bible Institute, and Master Charge would have been something experienced by head electricians. But here and there, black ink was showing up. New York's Bankers Trust lost, according to one report, $5.4 million in 1969, $3 million in 1970, but looked for a profit in 1971. First National City Bank of New York reported that its own credit card program was over the hump. And card bankers at California's Wells Fargo were finally smiling.

Some banks improved their card income just by changing the

way finance charges were levied. Even though annual interest rates were still restricted to from 12% to 18% in different states across the country, some bankers found ways to get those rates as high as 66%.

At the time, bank cards allowed from 25 to 45 days from the end of a monthly billing period for payment before adding finance charges. Most kept those "free" periods, but some found ingenious ways to up the interest rates for customers who chose to finance part of what they owed.

These were some of the various systems banks used to charge interest:

Adjusted balance. Customer pays interest on what is owed after all of the payments and credits on the bill have been subtracted from what was owed at the end of the month before.

Average daily balance. Payments are subtracted (or credits added) to the customer's account when they come in; then the daily balances are added up and divided by thirty, for days in the month. Anything bought on the card during this billing period is not included in these daily balances.

Before-payments balance. Customer pays interest on what is owed after any credits or adjustments are made, but before any payments are credited and subtracted.

Previous month's closing balance. Interest is figured out solely on what was owed the month before without subtracting any credits or payments.

For those cardholders who opted to take advantage of the card's cash-advance possibilities, the interest systems grew even more complicated, more rewarding to bankers. Because cash advances virtually never carry a free interest period, and because most banks add additional charges, the price of borrowing can be steep. With one system, in popular use, interest on the cash advance was based on the average-daily-balance system plus a 4% one-time charge on the loan. For cardholders who frequented this opportunity, the percentage rate could run up to that prohibitive 66% in the first month.

Other banks attacked their loss problems by cracking down on fraud, hiring newly trained experts in bank card operations, introducing new security measures throughout their systems. But even as these leaky seams were calked, liquid assets leaked out elsewhere. In one case, a young man used his smaller-limit bank card and got an authorized okay to buy a $250 motorcycle. He turned the motorcycle in on an expensive luxury car and disappeared. Nor were bankers in Arizona too swift when they said it was okay for a thief accused of bank card fraud to post his bail with . . . a bank card. He is also among the missing—and so is their money.

At Master Charge, some member banks attacked the problem of losses by weeding out their cardholder lists, cutting out unprofitable customers. One member bank cut its group by almost a third, ended up making more money.

Despite Dee Hock's literary-quarterly leadership, the Master Charge group outperformed the BankAmericard team in the early 1970's. Both cards in combination were taking over the country, were drastically changing the way Americans shopped and the way banks did business. By 1975 a cardholder could not only buy "just about everything just about everywhere," but could deposit or withdraw cash, transfer money among accounts, borrow money without ever appearing in a bank. These were some of the merchandising pluses enterprising banks had added to the bank card's capabilities through a form of computer terminal called automatic tellers. Located in airports, supermarkets, cafeterias, shopping centers, these automatic tellers gave banks unattended "branch offices" without the high costs of real estate, personnel, equipment, and other overhead. Some states that do not allow branch banking are still testing the legality of these locations and their services.

Bank cards also became respectable credit devices in many major department stores. Although these retailers had long fought the cards, preferring customers to use the store's own credit and interest-earning system, the overwhelming number of cards out dictated acceptance. By the end of 1976 giants like Weibolt's in Chicago, Gimbels and Korvettes in New York, Hecht Co. in Washington, D.C., and scores of others would accept Master Charge, BankAmericard, cash, checks, or their own cards for purchases.

Things looked good for the bank cards and their bankers in 1975. *The Nilson Report* said that Master Charge now had 37 million card carriers, was signed up with 1.2 million merchants, and cardholders spent $11.3 billion with the Interbank system that year. BankAmericard had 31.1 million cards out, 1.2 million merchants, and sales volume was $8.9 billion. Both outfits were developing highly advanced communications systems, were upgrading their advertising and marketing (NBI's plans to change BankAmericard to Visa were well underway), and people throughout the world were learning to use bank cards instead of checks or cash.

There was only one dark spot on the horizon, and it became a storm cloud that threatened to wash out the high-stepping parade.

A couple of years before, in 1973, a small but ambitious bank located in Little Rock had challenged the bank-card two-party system and American free enterprise. It was David, not against Goliath, but versus a panzer division. Officials at this organization, the Worthen Bank, decided that NBI was guilty of some form of trade restraint. What they were fighting was an NBI rule which said that card-issuing banks of that system were limited to BankAmericard and could not issue competing bank cards, such as Master Charge. The Interbank–Master Charge system had no rule about this with its banks, since the NBI rule automatically divided the nation's bank-card banks into one or the other system. Worthen filed a type of antitrust action against NBI, claiming it should be allowed to handle both cards.

It was like a Chevrolet dealer demanding the right to also sell Fords, a Burger Chef wanting to peddle Big Macs, a single motel offering a choice of Holiday Inn or TraveLodge accommodations.

Credit card bankers and their attorneys didn't take the case too seriously at first, but Worthen persisted. After years of wrangling and a series of unsatisfactory hearings, Hock and the NBI board of directors decided reluctantly to give up its ban on dual membership. Suddenly all BankAmericard banks were permitted to issue Master Charge cards and Interbank members to issue BankAmericards.

One controversial story said that Hock might very well have wanted it this way. The president of NBI had a well-earned reputation for "arranging" events to come out according to his personal master plan. One of his vice-presidents noted that, "Dee Hock plays his board of directors like Ohio State plays Coolidge High." Seemingly reluctant, the highly astute Hock knew that there were many more banks issuing Master Charges than BankAmericards and that BankAmericard could only improve its position with this move, which was termed "duality."

Instead of less, there was immediately more competition. Before duality, the fight was between banks which issued BankAmericard and those which offered Master Charge. With duality, every bank was against all others, departments within the banks were fighting, once-friendly executives were snarling at longtime associates and co-workers.

Since restrictions were off, banks began trying to increase their number of cardholders by invading other banks' customer lists. People who were carrying one BankAmericard from, say, First National Bank, suddenly received either an application for or a card from Second National Bank, and one from Third National Bank, all in the same city, plus one or two from banks outside that city, even outside that state. Applications came for additional BankAmericards to BankAmericard holders, plus applications for Master Charges, too. Master Charge carriers were swamped with the opportunity to add one, three, five BankAmericards to their porta-plastic collection. New cards, each with its own credit limit, meant dramatically increased spending possibilities. Some individuals, limited to $750 on one card, had a line of bank card credit in the thousands within weeks.

Dee Hock continued talking, this time in a discouraged tone. "What incentive is there to make one better or different from the other? Why should members support two systems, to compete, in effect, with themselves?" Meanwhile, member banks of the NBI system were watching the new cardholders sign up, watching the sales volume bubble upward.

Hock strolled the deep-carpeted, lush halls of NBI headquarters on a top floor of San Francisco architecture's black mark, the Bank of America Building, marking his steps by telling people to mark his words. Someday these two systems might become one, and that day, the antitrust people will either have to take legal action or put the bank-card system under federal regulation as a utility, he forecast.

Despite increased costs to handle the two systems within one organization, most banks scurried to issue or handle both cards. Even Wells Fargo, which had found that issuing a card bearing its archrival's name (BankAmericard) was "unpalatable," decided to join the blue-white-gold card to its already available red-yellow-circles one. Making the change a lot more palatable to Wells Fargo and other California banks was NBI's decision to change the card name to Visa. (That name change brought about bitter fights and a massive lawsuit—all detailed elsewhere in this book in Chapter 6.)

Either to get more cards on the street, or to avoid more antitrust action, or both, NBI began accepting organizations other than banks as card issuers. Savings-and-loan companies and credit unions were seriously considered by the board. Today, Visa cards are issued by quite a few organizations which have nothing to do with banking, such as the American Automobile Association.

There is one other bank card entity which received as much controversial attention as Dee Hock. It is New York's tough and aggressive Citicorp, owner of the mammoth Citibank. Bankers there seem pledged to make that institution a truly national bank. Already the largest issuer of Master Charge cards in 1977, Citibank began to build its new Visa card business by offering that card to an estimated 27 million people in twenty-five states, including such "greater New York" areas as Kentucky, Washington, and California.

Other bankers, outmaneuvered by Citibank in their own areas, began yelling foul, complaining that Citibank had deliberately and unfairly confused customers in its solicitation letter by saying, "Visa is replacing National BankAmericard." The implication was that BankAmericard was no longer good, especially to the tens of millions who may have been only dimly aware that BankAmericard was going through a name change.

Additional confusion was, as one banker noted, compounded daily, because most customers believed that there was only one Visa or BankAmericard or Master Charge or Master-Card where in actuality there were thousands of different kinds, varying in credit limits and systems, stemming from the more than 14,000 card-handling organizations. Most people who carry and use bank cards today still do not understand this. A Visa from Citibank is not the same as a Visa from Bank of America. What is the same is the look of the card and the fact that it can be used in all Visa card-accepting businesses. What can be totally different is what that card can do (automatic tellers, cash advances, etc.), interest rates and/or how they are figured, membership fees, transaction fees. The fact is that each bank is really in the card business for itself, belongs to the system mainly so its card can be accepted everywhere and so it can make money by handling billing for other banks' customers shopping in its area.

Citibank's controversial letter congratulated individuals on their fine credit rating and were mass-mailed to blue-ribbon housing tracts throughout California (among other states), offering the lucky receiver a choice of Master Charge or Visa card by simply filling out the enclosed form. Credit limits ranging up to $1,300 were based purely upon the economic standing of the tract or zip code. There were some odd results, including lower limits offered to some Bank of America and Visa executives than to many of their lesser-paid employees.

In one area, a young insurance salesman who had been limited to a $600 credit limit on his United California Bank Master Charge was suddenly offered a Citibank Master Charge with an $1,100 limit and a few weeks later, another with a $700 limit. That was before he had even received his quota of solicitations for Visa.

The demand for plastic blanks which get embossed and become bank cards was so great that one company, Data Card Corp., sold $34 million worth of them in the year ending March 25, 1978, and showed a hefty profit of $2.3 million. Someone must have been listening when Dustin Hoffman was advised to go into "plastics" in the motion picture *The Graduate*.

Big-city hype came to bank cards. Citibank began running nationwide contests, driving customers into the stores and conservative bankers into turbo-charged apoplexy. One contest offered such glistening temptations as a Mercedes-Benz and a twenty-one-day trip to Europe for two, plus a free $5,000 on the card. Another giveaway had a top prize of $5,000 to pay the winner's income taxes.

One banker close to Citicorp estimated that the organization had put together a $50 million marketing fund to build a cardholder base from New York to California and become a national bank not in name but in fact. According to that man, one of Citibank's largest plans is to set up the long-awaited and bitterly controversial Electronic Funds Transfer System (EFTS), which would eliminate checking accounts, credit cards, and replace most financial systems with a debit card and electronic processing, the eventual Lifebank system.

The debit card looks like a credit card, is carried like a credit card, is used like a credit card. Actually, it has no credit attached to it (except loans and cash advances in some places). With a debit card, when a customer buys a Sunbeam Mixmaster or a pair of designer jeans or a T-bone-for-two dinner, that card is inserted in an electronic terminal which tells the master computer to deduct the cost of the purchase from the customer's bank account right then and there and add it to the store/restaurant's account. There is no credit, no billing; a statement of purchases and balances comes to the customer at month's end. Because of its simplicity, the elimination of costly paperwork, the drastic reduction of fraud and credit-loss possibilities, it is the bankers' jackpot. Dee Hock once said EFTS is still "light-years away"; Citibank says we'll see about that. With highly developed EFTS, Citibank could easily and rapidly move ahead of Bank of America, become the largest bank in the nation to handle more people's financial affairs than any other organization.

With cards popping up bigger and better, like Orville Redenbacher's popcorn, there were about 92 million of them out by 1977 in the United States. Visa was playing catch-up, running approximately 3.8 million cards behind Master Charge. However, the overseas figures were different. Worldwide, Visa had over 58 million cards out, while Master Charge had a little over 57 million, according to an industry publication. Included in these totals were cards known under other names (Barclaycard of Great Britain, Carte Bleau of France, Chargex of Canada) that had joined the Visa lineup, and Access of Great

Britain, Eurocard International, and others that had signed up with Master Charge. For the first time, Visa's publicity folks began rattling their cages about worldwide leadership.

Dee Hock said, "It's a good horse race." Then he added, "We do not see Interbank as a worldwide competitor."

John Reynolds, then head of Interbank, responded, "We're still the Number One charge card used by more people to buy more things in more places than any other card. There is no doubt that we will maintain our lead." Which, as it turned out, falls into the cracked-crystal-ball category.

After some seven lean years, in early summer 1978 Visa officially announced that it was now number one worldwide. Elated and sassy, Hock called Interbank and Master Charge now number two and compared them to Avis, as the runner-up in the bank card business. Visa's spokesfolk also looked down their collective noses at Interbank's "clout" advertising campaign of the period and suggested that Master Charge might want to reconsider its no-longer-valid claim about "more people using it to buy more things . . ."

Visa's growth to the top shouldn't have been that surprising or unexpected to Master Charge bankers. While Master Charge had been growing impressively since 1975 and duality, Bank-Americard-Visa's growth had been extraordinary. And it continued. In January, February, and March 1978, Visa grew 60% over the same period in 1977, while Master Charge showed only a 30% increase for the same period.

In addition to duality, a talented staff of aggressive bank card experts, and new technologically advanced communications systems, one Visa executive credits the name change for much of the growth. "It's an exciting and glamorous name which holds much promise for the cardholder, is understood in all foreign countries, and besides, we spent 30% more on advertising it than Interbank did for Master Charge," he said. Then he added, "Having Citibank and Wells Fargo pushing Visa didn't hurt us either."

Meanwhile, back at Interbank, John Reynolds was still dismissing Visa's growth as "a one year kind of thing" and he commented about the "viciousness" of Visa's comments about Master Charge/Avis. "I don't care to get into that kind of war with them," he said. "He forgot he started it?" questioned one of Hock's staff.

A Master Charge sympathizer grudgingly said, "Visa's growing as though it's fertilized. You can read anything you want to into that comparison."

Reviewing its remarkable growth, Visa officials had to credit its rapid and complete domination of the foreign bank card/ credit card potential as a major contributor. In line with Hock's long-held dream of a truly international card which operated under one name and one set of standards, Visa easily outdistanced Interbank and its affiliates overseas.

In late 1972, an international committee of people from NBI membership and foreign card organizations licensed by the Bank of America began looking at the idea of a multinational corporation. That group was named Ibanco, and in October 1974 it began accepting charter members. Its objectives were to increase card acceptance and usage throughout the world and to develop electronic data-processing systems to provide better international service to banks, cardholders, and merchants. Originally, members issued blue-white-gold BankAmericard-type cards with their own names on them. Later, cards were converted to carry the name Visa in the white band. If Barclaycard wanted to use its name also, that went in the blue band. Only cards that were used inside one country were not required to carry the Visa logo. Ibanco was a coming together of the scattered, unorganized bank card/credit card movement overseas.

One of the first cards to be introduced in Europe had been the BankAmericard-type Barclaycard, sponsored by Great Britain's largest banking institution, Barclays. It was not a good time for cards in Great Britain. Trying to stop the devaluation of the pound, the Labor government put heavy restrictions on credit, discouraging use of the card. Too, staid Britishers who hadn't warmed up much to earlier imports like Diners Club and American Express also sniffed at the Barclaycard.

At about the same time, in the late 1960's, Interbank went aggressively after business in Japan and Western Europe. It had already signed up the important Banco Nacional de Mexico, S.A. Actually, Japan, not a frontier country for credit cards, had its own system established in 1960 when Diners, Fuji Bank, and the Japan Travel Bureau had put one together. However, BankAmericard moved into competition later, signed up Sumitomo Bank in Japan, and also four Chargex banks in Canada. That was the beginning.

By late 1979 the largest system, Visa, was good for the money in 130 countries, the blue-white-gold stripes more recognized by many people on the street than their own flags. Worldwide, it had 80 million cardholders.

Once again, communication was a major part of Visa's success. That organization's electronic whizzes had put together an international authorization system which could give a purchase okay within four seconds.

For Interbank, there was not good news at home, either. Early in 1979, the country's third largest bank, Chase Manhattan, informed tens of thousands of its Master Charge holders that the bank would no longer handle that card. They were advised to cut them up and switch to Visa. The glee club met at Visa headquarters, and one happy executive said, "The competitive war ebbs and flows, but boy oh boy, are things ever flowing in our direction."

Chase Manhattan bankers had made that decision based on a New York state law that calls for combining a customer's outstanding balances which, in effect, cuts down the amount of interest the bank can charge on each account. Later, other banks began cutting back on one or both cards. It was an audible rumbling on the earthquake faults running through the bank card business.

If it wasn't recession or depression, it was credit and fraud loss. If it wasn't high start-up costs and bad management, it was the increasingly prohibitive cost of money. From the beginning of the bank card business, the industry had faced a series of financial problems. Duality was no different, bringing its own Pandora's cash register. The cost of carrying two separate but almost identical card programs, tied in with the high cost of money, was driving expenses up. Limited to state-mandated annual interest charges and paying extraordinary (for banks) interest rates for outside money, bank card officers were caught between the rock and hard-cash place. Then, adding in the losses from bad credit and fraud, some bankers even decided to forgo the business and go off to New England and raise Christmas trees.

Duality had created much of this problem for the banks, just as it created overspending permissiveness for the cardholders. By the end of 1979 the bank cards were putting a significant number of the people who used them and the banks who handled them into important debt. The only seemingly satisfied people were those card carriers who paid off their balances promptly and who used the cards as a pleasant, free convenience and some merchants who found that the cards had increased their business even though they had to raise prices to cover the discount kickback to the bank.

Dee Hock summed up Visa's position in duality during a speech he made at a late-1979 bank-card convention: "Members [banks] may incur the inefficiencies and costs of operating two different programs without competitive advantage or reward . . . when you hold both rapiers, the duel is between your right and left hand, and the blood shed your own!"

At the same meeting, Donald L. Baker, who had been an Assistant Attorney General for Antitrust, added, "Bank cards . . . are evolving so fast that the problems will not be your grandchildren's or even your children's problems to solve . . . they are already yours."

When the duality situation happened, the secondary fighting between the two systems almost vanished and was replaced with fighting between individual banks to see who could issue the most cards, get the most people in debt. With total consumer debt about $1.2 trillion and increasing in leaps of 15.5% a year, as it did in 1979, there were only two things that could happen. People would stop spending. When that happens, it's a depression. Or if unemployment increased, millions of people would not pay their debts, worsening a depression. There is a third option, and that is increased spending and consumer debt, and that way lies only more crippling inflation. All three happened in 1980.

By the end of 1979, every man, woman, and child in this country was in lowercase hock for about $6,000 and every household owed 85% of its income after taxes. This was total debt, not bank card debt alone, but as one Washington politician noted, "The banks, who are supposed to be our good examples, not only encouraged us to get in over our heads, but they provided the plastic shovel to dig that hole. So what are they doing now that we have a crisis in personal and national finances, they're yelling 'foul' because they got in the hole, too. Now we're all in trouble."

Bank cards had come a long, frightening way.

6

Hot Air and Cold Cash

PEOPLE ARE CREATURES of habit, and it is not easy to change them. But it can be done. At first, the new instant cake mixes were sneered at by the nation's homemakers. Today, a cake made from scratch is neighborhood news. Jeans were once the uniforms of cowboys, railroad brakemen, stevedores. Now they are worn to opening night at the opera. There are hundreds of examples.

The difference is advertising. The effect of billions of dollars behind thousands of cunningly persuasive messages has totally changed the ways we eat, dress, travel, and now, the way we handle our money. The greatest single influence in changing us from a conservative, thrift-minded people to money-tossing spendthrifts has been bank card advertising. After all, if those legendarily tight-fisted bankers have been smilingly encouraging us to buy-buy-buy (with their money!), it must be all right, because surely they must know what they're doing?

Traditionally, this society has lived with the difficult choice of spending its money or saving it. High productivity backed by mass marketing methods has made possible reasonably priced new cars, gourmet foods, two-TV homes, overseas vacations for tens of millions. Consumer luxuries like eleven-function digital watches, home computers, stereos with the power of small stations, champagne at beer prices, surround our natural and created needs, tug at both our heart and purse strings.

But we are also a people raised on the work ethic and have been trained by our conservative parents, by an uneven economic past, and by our institutions (including especially our banks!) to save money as much as possible. For working people this was hard, but the American Way demanded that we put something aside to buy a house, to send the kids to college, to be independent in our old age.

But saving is no fun. And spending is. If the banks' advertising not only says it's okay but actually shows us how to do it, guilt disappears. The instant cake mix is delicious, the jeans are perfect for a job interview, and we've changed our mind about what to do with our money, too. People who once wouldn't spend a dollar for an all-day streetcar pass now spend thousands for a week in Hawaii. The meat-and-potatoes man now demands filet and soufflé. There are more Cadillacs sold in some lower socio-economic neighborhoods than Fords. And the bankers smiled and nodded and continued dealing from the bottom of their marked deck.

They knew better, the bankers did. They knew that going into burdensome debt was a violation of all sound financial principles for the person, for the family. Yet they continued pushing the cards, pushing debt, using the incredible weight of multimillion-dollar advertising budgets to encourage our national spending binge. We were painting the town red and we were all going into the red doing it.

Originally, all advertising was innocent in its intent. It was purely a notice that something was for sale. When bank cards first came about, advertising notified us that there existed a new plastic miracle which could make our lives easier, more organized, and more comfortable. During the middle years of the 1970's, advertising was used to recruit new card carriers and to promote continued, steady use of the cards. Today, bank-card advertising concentrates almost solely on the card for just about every possible purchase, every available banking service.

Back in the middle 1960's, when each bank or small group of banks had its own card and there were no national hookups like Visa or MasterCard, advertising was all over the place, literally (one bank-card campaign appeared on posters inside men's-room toilet doors). Cards were advertised like headache remedies ("Fast financial relief!"), like deodorants ("Be socially acceptable, be secure"), like sanitary napkins ("For those monthly problems"). "Greed and Need!" barked one bank executive to his ad agency. "Appeal to both!" he ordered.

It was each bank for itself, and highly paid professional communicators outdid each other to get their particular plastic into empty hands. Many advertisements and commercials were tasteless, misleading, frightening. One bank spot showed a man dressed like a gangster pulling a card out of a shoulder holster and palming it like a gun while scurrying clerks piled goods on the counter for him. Another appealed to guilt by showing tearful tykes waiting for a Santa Claus who might not come this year. Some of this type of advertising was attacked by civic leaders, by state legislators, even by the generally self-protective advertising industry itself.

By the time National BankAmericard Incorporated and Interbank were fairly well organized in 1971, one of their main jobs was to straighten out the advertising for the bank cards.

It was not an easy assignment. Both groups faced the double job of creating advertising which had an overall national look and theme but which gave options so that member banks could use it or continue their own. Before any kind of advertising could be developed, certain facts had to be faced, facts which were coming out through advertising and marketing research.

One of these search processes is called advertising-copy research. It is a system dreamed up by advertising people to second-guess themselves. They have expensive companies go out and ask people what they would like to hear. Then the advertising writers and creative people are told to repeat what the researchers say people want to hear. It is a system soothing and comforting to ad executives because it appears fail-safe ("After all, J.G., research said that's what people wanted").

The process has two major flaws. The first is that people do not know what they want to hear until they hear it. They tend to repeat yesterday's ads until a new idea comes along, and then they go with that one. Approached by a researcher and asked for your idea of the perfect automobile ad, you would probably not say, "Lemon." Yet, that is probably the most

95

memorable ad for Volkswagen (or any car) ever created. What you probably would parrot is, "Dependable, Reasonable, Beautiful," or some such, because that has been your major experience with car advertising.

The second flaw in copy researching is that new news becomes old news fast. If that same researcher stopped you and said, "Would you describe the bank card as a total revolution in banking?" you would probably try to be agreeable and say yes. The researcher would report back that you (and others) feel that way, and the creative folk are ordered to write the ads that way. The problem is that those ads don't work, and everyone wanders around scratching various parts of his body and wondering where it went wrong. Everyone but the good creative people. They are not surprised at all. Intuition and understanding of people are part of their job, and they know that people do not think that way, that bankers think that way. "What we should have said instead of 'a revolution in banking,' which is self-serving drool for bankers," says the copywriter, "was, 'The next time you're out of cash, you're not out of money.' That's a message people can understand." The writer is correct, of course.

However, even the most creative writer and all other advertising people can use *general* market research. This is factual data which help picture who is out there, what they need, how they feel, how to reach them. Highly trained probers, some with doctorates in locating your internal triggers, began finding ways to put cards into America's life-style.

Early market research showed that card carriers of the time or ripe candidates for cards fell into one of three target groups. They were the Undecideds, the Marginals, and the Users. If you were an Undecided, you wanted the convenience of credit but were afraid of debt. If you were a Marginal, you carried a bank card but seldom if ever used it. If you were a User, you could be either a heavy or a light one. The job of bank-card advertising was to get all three of these groups to carry cards and to get those cards used more.

The best way to get to the Undecideds, the mass manipulators decided, was emergencies. A flat tire. An unexpected illness. Running out of cash. These were reasons everyone should have a card. They knew that once the card was used for an emergency, the Undecided would start creating emergencies like January White Sales to use it again.

For the Marginals, who already carried a card, advertising was constructed to the Good Life appeal. Why wait, enjoy IT today. Take that trip, buy that suit, get the car fixed now, while you can enjoy it, while you need it, before it costs more.

For the Users, most of whom showed up as higher-educated, higher-income individuals, the sophisticated advantages of the card were promoted. Money management, budgeting, pay-all-bills-with-one-check, built-in tax records, were some of the advantages sold to this group to encourage wider and more frequent use of the card.

The first truly coordinated BankAmericard national advertising campaign with which local banks could tie in was sent forth by NBI in 1971; it pushed the slogan "Think of it as money." That theme was paired with the illustration of a BankAmericard inside a coin-bearing money clip.

For the Undecideds, the Marginals, the Users, the message had been carefully constructed; there's nothing frightening or mysterious about this plastic card—it's just your good old friend *money* in a more convenient form. The motivational researchers thought it perfect. For the Undecideds, the card was not debt, but cash. For the Marginals, it was emergency credit, but that was morally okay. For the Users, it was a reassurance that regular card spending was the smart thing to do.

At about this same time, the Master Charge banks were still using trite-but-true old advertising and promotional devices. For example, New York's Chemical Bank was trying to get out the vote by offering discount coupons for card users. Car-rental outfits, tire stores, restaurants, and other merchants chipped in to this type of promotion, and card carriers were encouraged to "save over $100" by using the card and the coupons.

Some banks hitchhiked on the national advertising campaigns and some continued running their own appeals. One bank is reported to have run an ad headlined "We'll carry you longer than your mother did," but didn't bother to mention that Mom didn't charge 18% annual interest for the term. Others went for the new plastic snobbery with lines like "Give yourself credit for spending wisely." Still others went heavily into scare tactics with appeals like "Don't be caught short when you take the boss to dinner," or "Your wife has a flat tire on a dark, lonely road, and no cash!"

Although "Think of it as money" and its later suggested replacement, "More than money," were noncontroversial, safe, well-researched themes, they were also as flat as a newly printed dollar. In 1973, NBI's president, Dee Hock, decided that he wanted a new advertising agency. The large national group which had worked with them since the formation of NBI had never been accepted by some influential bank members of that organization because it also handled part of Bank of America's advertising. Too, NBI headquarters were located in the Bank of America Building, and there was a belief among those banks that B of A had too much single influence on BankAmericard advertising and marketing.

Dee Hock had a native distrust of advertising people. He tended to believe that they were overdressed and overpaid and overly self-impressed, that they took marathon liquor-soaked lunches, and that they made a living by manipulating not only the public but also the advertisers who paid the bills.

Operating out of these beliefs, and also afraid of police action on BankAmericard advertising from legislative groups, he had drawn up a forbidding list of Do's and Don'ts for advertising. These were known as The Creative Commandments, here somewhat edited for space and comprehension:

1. The idea or theme must be fresh enough to last for two or three years so it gains strength through repetition yet should be flexible enough to carry variations.

2. There must be a natural place in the advertising for local banks to be identified with the message.

3. The theme should be so strong that local banks can change it as much as they want without destroying it.

4. It should also be flexible enough to carry any message from hard sell to low key approaches.

5. It should also be flexible enough to change as the product changes without losing the theme or the impression already made upon the public.

6. It must appeal to all ages and mentalities but not be insulting to the most intelligent or a putdown to the dumbest.

7. It must establish (our card) as the top card in the credit card field.

8. It must work hand in hand with a total public relations program.

9. It must form the base for educational programs and materials.

10. It must relate well to overall legislative problems and objectives, helping to resolve anti-credit card legal problems.

11. It must be so individually addressed people feel it is written to them personally yet . . .

12. . . . handle within its scope far-reaching, all-encompassing economic and social trends.

13. It must position (our card) with solid, constructive virtues.

14. It must be usable in print, on radio, in TV, on outdoor boards, for mailers, posters, inside the banks.

15. It must be able to handle all product differences whether the individual banks have cash dispensing machines, tax payment checks, cash advances, different interest rates, etc.

16. It must work with local bank advertising themes.

17. It must not be constructed to appeal to any particular area of the country, the state, city, or the world.

18. It can have no brag-and-boast (biggest, best, No. 1).

19. It must not be misleading or depart from the truth.

20. It must not violate any regulations.

21. It should not be created to win advertising prizes.

22. It should not fight directly with themes of other cards or advertising from other financial institutions.

23. It must produce better results for less advertising money.

Operating within those rules, or variations of them down through the NBI years, Hock felt he had a tight rein on the craziness or irresponsibility which had characterized a great deal of bank card advertising.

Experienced copywriters, those who have wrestled for years with the impossible regulations controlling liquor and pharmaceutical ads (two of the highly controlled areas), agreed that the demands made by Hock certainly locked in the assignment and the creative mind as well.

In 1973, after firing its advertising agency, NBI became the

Eldorado of hungry other firms. (Most did not know of Hock's forbidding manifesto.) An advertising account like Bank-Americard was considered a showpiece account for an agency. It was a high-profile advertiser with commercials and ads on view to multimillions. It was a good- and prompt-paying account. Despite the choking restrictions of the Command-ments, creative people could possibly do something good without dealing in cents off coupons or six-for-a-dollar appeals. That year, NBI was projecting some $4-million-plus for its own BankAmericard advertising, which meant a healthy income of $400–$600,000 for the ad agency. Overall, including NBI's spending, plus other individual bank efforts, the push for that card was estimated at over $13 million for the year.

An elimination contest was started. Over a dozen agencies of all sizes were reviewed, including nationally famous ones like Cunningham & Walsh, and BBD&O, plus smaller local organi-zations. At that time, no one realized the end result of that search for a new agency would be a complete and dramatic shift in the personality and fortunes of BankAmericard.

A small, select group of finalists was chosen by the advertis-ing manager, top administrative executives of NBI, and the director of communications. These agencies were given a complete backgrounding on the bank card business, and were asked to come in with a recommended advertising program and campaign. Part of the suggested assignment was a name change for the card, theoretically to see what could be done with a new piece of plastic instead of depending upon con-ditioning from past campaigns. To cover part of their out-of-pocket expenses, each finalist agency would be given a fairly hefty check. The idea of having them do work on a hypothetical new card was not that far removed from need. Future planners at NBI were aware many other banks in the system didn't care much about promoting a card with another bank's name (B of A) on it and realized the day would come when a name change might be needed.

Although all of the agencies were given the same informa-tion, the same figures, the same assignment, the same warn-ings, some of their dog-and-pony shows turned out to be just dogs.

One large agency with a branch office in San Francisco, NBI's headquarters town at the time, thought so highly of their work and their chances, they involved the top echelon of their New York office in the work and the presentation. The New York Scheherazade flown out to do the spiel was professional, slick, well-prepared. Unfortunately, his material wasn't. To the increasing disbelief of the conservative bankers and marketing people from NBI, he proudly dramatized a suggested commercial. In that spot, a man was shoveling himself into a very deep pit. When he was so far down he couldn't climb out, the announcer said something like, "When you get in a hole (or over your head) let BankAmericard get you out," at which point a BankAmericard was thrown into the hole as a lifesaving ladder device.

The concept of associating BankAmericard with "getting into a hole" and with crushing debt was as appealing to the reviewing group as a bank failure. And to top if off, the agency had not truly followed the assignment, had not come up with a new name for a card. That agency, on a scale of one to ten, scored minus three. Later, when one of its executives was told his agency had not been selected, he became miffed, returned the check NBI had sent along to cover presentation expenses, and demanded the right to sell the idea to Interbank. If it ever showed up on Master Charge spots, it didn't leave a lasting impression.

The other finalists came in with advertising layouts, sketches, radio commercials, television storyboards, mailers, fliers, posters, bus cards, and with heavily displayed sincerity, dedication, loyalty, creativity, marketing, media programs, and research studies all spilling over onto tables, chairs, easels, the floor. The advertising trade press kettledrummed it up as the most exciting thing that had happened in advertising since the Noxzema take-it-off girl. One noted female executive of a large national agency threatened to check into a Motel 6 in the area and stay there until her agency got the business.

"I don't believe you can get a motel room for six dollars these days," one of NBI's top men commented joshingly.

"Come over tonight and I'll show you . . ." she invited.

Another female from a competing but much smaller West

Coast agency wasn't as interested in the presentations as she was in what the other female was wearing. When told it was an expensive designer suit, she showed up to do her turn in unpressed jeans and a knit shawl. The circus went on.

Then, at one point, a medium-sized San Francisco-based agency came in, did its number, waited for reactions.

"Did the earth move for you?" one of the NBI executives asked another.

"Was it good for you too?" was the reply.

That agency had presented work so well-thought-out, so solidly based, so carefully planned, and so creatively on target that it drew not applause but a hushed and respectful silence.

There, glistening in the middle of the barge-long conference table, was a mock-up of a blue-white-gold-striped card. It looked exactly like a BankAmericard but it had a different name on it.

It said "Visa."

A spokesman for the agency pointed out that they had undertaken the suggested assignment to change the card name. He added that the word "Visa" was one of the few pronounced the same and with the same meaning throughout the world, that it meant travel but it also meant an opening, an entrance, a passport to things new.

On chairs, on easels, on the walls, on the table, there were suggested commercials, ads, mailers, and other advertising carriers with assorted messages built around the name and the idea of Visa.

That agency was so on the mark, seemed to know so much about NBI's upcoming but still secret needs, there was later suspicion that someone at NBI had coached them along conspiratorially so that they would get the job.

Their work was a home run, a touchdown, a three-point basket, all in one. They got the account, the advertising work for NBI.

And then the trouble started.

Since the concept for Visa couldn't be used for a couple of years (if ever) while Bank of America was being paid out by members of NBI for use of that system, the agency was asked to come up with another campaign. What it came up with was a camp or a pain but not a workable campaign, not to the advertising decision makers at NBI.

Several ideas were hastily sketched out on rough tissue paper. Representative of the group was a suggested commercial which featured dancer Ray Bolger performing in a shopping-mall street while singing the song "Me and My Shadow" with new purchase-oriented lyrics. The "shadow" of course was his BankAmericard. Its major crime was violation of NBI marketing's unwritten rule number one, which said no Bank-Americard advertising should blatantly push buying. That was and always has been the basic difference between Bank-Americard advertising and that of Master Charge. The MC card's advertising consistently sold consumption, acquisition, and spending.

When the NBI advertising manager and the director of communications asked to see the head of that agency to discuss disappointment with the new work, he responded in an unusual fashion. Instead of volunteering to have his people do more work until it was suitable for NBI, he lashed out, demanded that the director of communications of NBI be fired. When he was flatly and roundly turned down by startled NBI executives, including Dee Hock, he stalked out, saying, in essence, that they didn't want that old account anyway.

It all happened so fast—within two weeks or so—that when he exited stage left in an eight-cylinder huff, it wasn't clear who owned the name Visa. That was to lead to a major and critical lawsuit later.

An agency firing a client, especially one with a good product and high visibility and excellent payment record, created news not only in the advertising trade papers but also in the general press. It was the biggest thing to happen in the bank card business since the Chicago mail-drop disaster.

NBI had to move fast; its advertising plans for the upcoming seasons were badly behind schedule. NBI reviewed some other agencies that had made the original presentations, looked at additional ones, and finally decided to go another way. Dee Hock gave permission to his marketing people to bring the advertising activities within the company instead of hiring an outside firm. Talented experts were recruited, space was found, and NBI Communications was born, as an "in-house" agency.

Now, in-house operations offer their companies the major advantage of returning the 15% commissions that magazines, newspapers, broadcast, and other mediums pay to advertising agencies. On a budget of $4 million, the return would be $600,000; on a budget of $8 million, it becomes $1.2 million. It is more than enough to staff, equip, and rent space for a small (eight to ten people) agency. And to return a very handsome profit. Of course, the major disadvantage of an in-house agency is that the client is also the boss, and a healthy disagreement over creative approaches to a commercial could get a person demoted or fired.

For Hock, as boss-client, it was ideal. He could read his Creative Commandments, insert all of his personal advertising ideas, and be fairly sure that rapt attention was being paid to him and them.

NBI Communications was born during a tough time for bank cards. Many people were convinced that bank cards increased retail prices and contributed heavily to inflation. Long before the experts began pointing out these facts, the man-in-the-mall realized it. In addition, half the people didn't know whether bank cards were free or charged a membership fee, and three out of four believed that the card couldn't be used at all without paying finance charges. One out of two people also thought they were responsible for unlimited fraudulent charges if the card was lost or stolen, despite a great deal of publicity about legislation which limited responsibility to little or nothing.

Those misunderstandings and fears had to be eliminated by advertising and other communications. Along with a great deal of misunderstanding of the bank cards by the public, there was also a high degree of misunderstanding of the public by bank-card people.

Some startling new facts showed that things were changing out there in Consumerland. The traditional target for advertising, the main man to convince, had been the middle-aged, middle-income white-collar executive or professional. That group was the strength of the card business. Suddenly, research showed that salaries and wages of blue-collar workers were going way up and that more and more housewives were

104

working. At that time, figures showed that in addition to the 54% of all single women who worked, some 49% of married women had jobs. Here were two ripe new fields for the bank cards, millions of crops of new spenders just waiting to be harvested.

Advertising that had once been aimed at insurance salesmen or computer operators, doctors or draftsmen, was redesigned to set its cap for factory foremen and crane operators and carpenters and repairmen, electricians, cops, postal workers. When someone at a meeting said, "What about plumbers?" someone else answered, "With their income they've been on our white-collar list for years."

In advertising polytalk, these groups were known as "targets of opportunity," and the admen were out to get them all.

Computers are used by advertising people like a rigger uses a crane, like a carpenter uses a rule. Sophisticated analyses of the market came together in an "intermedia-behavior-patterns-by-quintiles/tertiles" study calculated to catch you in a withering crossfire of advertising. The ambitious program was carefully assembled so that local banks could reinforce the advertising pressure in local newspapers, on local radio, on billboards, even on painted bus benches.

At Interbank, Master Charge set out to sell you its card. If you were a home putterer, there was a huge promotion in *House & Garden* magazine which prodded you to remodel and put it on your Master Charge. If you were more interested in travel, *Esquire* magazine carried a special section on nine dream vacations that could come true if you rubbed your plastic MC genies.

Both bank cards, through the local banks, began pushing bonuses of the cards. You could get the advantages of an overdraft account which allowed you to spend even more than before, twenty-four-hour cash-dispensing machines so you could borrow when the banks were closed, another free bank card with a package account, so you could up your limits.

During the recession/depression of 1974–1975, the advertising decision makers at Interbank decided to change the Master Charge campaign from emphasis on spending to the card's role as a "money manager." It was planned to help cool down your spending, to help stop inflation, and to help the banks get their card business on a more settled, more profitable basis. It was a nice shot, but no cigar. Getting people to change their credit card habits was almost impossible. It was fun to spend money, right? And going back to the old virtues of thrift, saving, and economy was like going back to iceboxes. It was a drippy idea. That campaign became known as "the invisible one," because, as one Master Charge banker said, "Nobody could see it."

Meanwhile, back at BankAmericard, Dee Hock and his board of directors had decided to drop the name BankAmericard officially and replace it with Visa throughout the world. It was not like going to court to change your name from Sam to Charley. This changeover, including new cards, new decals for stores, other new equipment, plus advertising and other costs, was estimated to run from $10 to $20 million, all of which would have to be paid for in some way by you and the other card carriers. A careful timetable was put together which covered two years from first announcement of the Visa name to complete new identity.

To tell the world about it, NBI/Visa put together an ambitious advertising campaign, jacked its budget up a hefty amount, and threw the job to both its in-house agency and a newly appointed outside company, one of the agency business's oldies but not necessarily goodies. Having seen what San Francisco had to offer in the way of advertising agencies during the 1973 presentation when it changed shops, NBI/Visa went to Los Angeles for this one.

That didn't sit too well with San Francisco ad agencies. Especially one. That was the organization which had suggested the name Visa, the one whose head man had taken his jump rope and gone home when NBI wouldn't skip his way. Whether it was deliberate or not, the agency waited awhile to take action, a period in which NBI had committed heavily to the new changeover of name. This time the agency's creative idea wasn't Ray Bolger dancing in a shopping mall, but a heavy lawsuit aimed at NBI and its worldwide organization, Ibanco.

The lawsuit said, in so many words, that the name Visa had been created by them, had been more or less stolen from them, and that they wanted to be paid for it. It was difficult to decide how much, so the suit asked the court to assess the damages.

One involved person suggested that NBI/Ibanco be made to pay one percent of its sales volume for ten years. For 1977 alone, based on $15 billion on sales slips and cash advances, that would have rounded out nicely at $150 million. The name Visa, at that rate, could have been more valuable than that of Rockefeller or Rothschild.

Legally, NBI/Visa/Ibanco was sitting with a pretty good hand up, a pair of aces underneath. First, its attorneys felt the name had been "paid for" with the check the agency received to cover its speculative work in the presentation. Next, the agency had been hired in good faith based upon its work, had been offered payment, and it was the agency that had walked out on the relationship. Both written and unwritten general custom in advertiser-agency relationships is that all work done for the advertiser and paid for by the advertiser belongs to the advertiser.

To top it off, Visa's legal strong cards consisted of two pieces of homework done earlier. Visa had conducted a federal-trademark search and found that there was no problem there. And having located a small banking organization in another state which had been using the name for a long time for another banking service, NBI made arrangements with that group to obtain the name.

Finally, the Visa attorneys could argue that Visa was a common word, in the public domain, and really nobody's property. Playing safe, they registered it for financial services.

After two years of increasing the standard of living for many attorneys, the named and the nameless got together over the big V. For a nominal sum of money, the agency dropped the suit. Both sides agreed to keep the final settlement more secret than a bank-vault combination.

The sigh of relief from Visa officials was a 4.5 on the Richter scale. That name was the core center and the pivot around which BankAmericard was developing its new image, its new marketing, its new growth and expansion plans. Plain old BankAmericard had been sold and accepted as a drab, every-day plastic for buying clothes, furniture, gasoline. The glamorous ring of Visa sounded like a suite at the George V, opening night at La Scala, a pitside seat for a Grand Prix race.

New research showed that travel and entertainment was where the new and better profits were.

And Visa's Hocksters were out to get that market.

Visa people had known for a long time that although they had more cards out, people who were carrying Diners, Carte Blanche, and especially American Express were spending more each time they used those cards. By getting people to run up higher bills with a bank card, the finance fees could be much more rewarding for the banks.

One advertising expert estimates that Visa spent 8–10 million dollars within six months to announce its new name. That heavy investment could have been one of the devices the "wronged" agency felt could force Hock to pay up. It didn't work.

The first Visa advertising, not a dramatic change from the old, continued to show people using cards in domestic situations and said, "We're keeping up with you." That line was carefully constructed to reassure you that although the world was changing, Visa would stand by your hip and see you through.

What was also slyly built into that line was the soothing lullaby to calm your fear of the dark when the bankers make their big move to get rid of checks, to go flat out into the computer-driven future of electronic money. By saying, "We're keeping up with you," the Hocksters were slyly saying that you asked us to do it for you, that we're just trying to help. Do you recall asking the bankers to take over your money, your finances, your paycheck, your income and outgo completely? Did you ask for Lifebank? That advertising campaign implied so.

For a long time, Master Charge advertising had been built around its number-one position. For years, it had more merchants, more card carriers, more dollars rung up on its sales slips. Then, in competing with BankAmericard and Visa plus American Express and the other travel-and-entertainment cards, Master Charge insisted that it had "clout." Clout, in its most noted American form, was a word used in Chicago to describe somebody's importance. For example, if that city's late Mayor Daley sent you a Christmas gift, you had clout. "Clout" also means a heavy hit or a blow that would send you reeling. One funster insisted that Master Charge's real clout was the interest rate on the monthly bills.

In the spring of 1979, Master Charge adfolk finally discovered that women were card users too. This followed by some ten years Carte Blanche's similar discovery, which resulted in issuing special pink-colored cards for women. Master Charge set out more than $3 million from its 1979 advertising to attempt selling that Chicago-political-machine word to the gentle sex. "My own job. My own clout," was the theme. The role models with which ladies were to identify included a film director, an airline pilot, an architect; all common, highly identifiable female occupations?

About a year later, in early 1980, Master Charge tardily followed NBI into a name change, but not much of one. Master Charge became MasterCard, because, as one of their executives declared, "The word charge just didn't go over in foreign countries." The new advertising had no hesitation about dragging you into tomorrow's electronic economy, just blurted it right out. "A subtle name change, but it will mean a world of possibilities for you," said the new ads. "And the Good Life. Because MasterCard is *becoming a system for universal transactions. For banking needs and services.*" Whose? Yours or theirs?

Visa approached 1980 advertising in another way. The campaign for the decade's beginning was carefully detailed, carefully scheduled, carefully crafted to help shoo away its five-and-dime image, to develop a new personality as everyman's American Express. "Your world is waiting, and Visa is there" was the promise. That promise was accompanied by those snappy fast-cut commericals which showed you and people like you living in the fast lane of luxurious travel, expensive shopping, gluttonous dining. Everyone was smiling, grinning, laughing, chortling, knocking himself out with joy, probably because the tab, the bill, the bottom line, was never mentioned, never showed up.

That was deliberate. The hundreds of millions of dollars spent on bank card advertising was not intended to promote thrift and budgeting and saving. The bank-card admen are not people of good deeds. Despite "go-slow" appeals in rough times, their job was to encourage spending—much and often—with the bank cards. The messages were cunningly contrived to build your appetites, to assure you that these luxuries were yours for the asking, and to provide the method for getting them. There was no mandatory warning on the cards that said, *Caution. Financial experts have determined that continued bank card use can lead to debt, loss of property, bankruptcy, plus unhealthful effects on long-lived standards and virtues.* But there should have been.

When credit controls came in, these programs were temporarily halted and some halfhearted attempts at "public-service" advertising were tried. In one flight of commercials, Interbank's new president, a man with the interesting name of Hogg for the credit business, cautioned card carriers to use their MasterCards sparingly. Once again, there was more than met the tube-oriented eye. While appearing to express concern for the cardholder's welfare, the commercials also helped discourage use of the Interbank cards with their then-dwindling profitability. Other financial institutions followed along similar lines. The prognosis for this concern-oriented approach was an early death. It was purely a time-buyer while the associations waited for the bad publicity on credit to blow away and for the bankers to start making brand-new profits with brand-new types of charges. At the same time, the T&E cards moved swiftly to take advantage of the bank card advertising hibernation. American Express ran advertisements assuring us that its card was not a credit device but a convenience. Diners Club hit harder. One full-page advertisement crowed, "Diners Club Has Seen the Bank Cards Come. Now We're Seeing Them Go."

The bankers, meanwhile, began revising existing campaigns to reflect more of a we-care-about-you approach. But they never lost sight of the advertising appeals that had sold you the reflex use of the card.

For the future as in the past, these friendly advertisements threw a comradely arm about your shoulder, passed a warm wink, and eagerly assured you that not only the good material things of life but also love, friendship, togetherness, and happiness could be yours if you'd just continue using your card today. Tomorrow? The day the bills come due? In bank-card advertising, my friend, tomorrow never comes.

It's a wry twist on the old tale of Hamelin. In the original, the Pied Piper took the kids because he wasn't paid, and led them to a hill where they disappeared. In the current version, the well-paid advertising pipers were leading us all to that mountain of debt where our savings, our security, our personal and national financial independence were all going to vanish.

7

Getting You on Line and in Line

HAVE YOU USED one of those automatic cash-dispensing machines? You put your bank card in, punch the amount you want (or can get), and prest-o, your financial condition is change-o. Or, how about those computer-driven automatic tellers, the bank industry's dream employee? Works twenty-four hours a day in all weather; never needs lunch or a trip to the restroom; makes loans, takes deposits, makes transfers, does just about everything a human teller can do except ask for a raise. In the electronics-communications business, these are known as *transaction terminals.*

You've undoubtedly also done bank card business with an electronic cash register or similar device used increasingly in stores and retail outlets to identify you, check your credit, charge the purchase, and help the clerk ring up the sale. Or one of those check-guarantee contraptions. These miracles of monetary manipulation are called *point-of-sale terminals.*

Both transaction terminals and point-of-sale terminals are a crucial part of complex, advanced electronic systems which begin with you and your bank card and will end with Lifebank. Sort of, the tithe that binds.

Every time you use one of these terminals or somebody else does, you and they are helping to build, enlarge, and strengthen rapid worldwide financial communications, the one lifeline which Lifebank must have to operate.

This system has many names: electronic banking, paperless banking, electronic money, data communications, electronic value exchange, electronic transfer, and even the cashless society. The bankers call it electronic funds-transfer systems (EFTS), or just plain EFT.

Defining EFT so everyone would be agreed on what it was became the job of a national commission appointed by Congress in 1974. That commission finally Washingtoned, "[EFT] is a payments system in which the processing and communications necessary to effect economic exchange and the processing and communications necessary for the production and distribution of services incidental or related to economic exchange are dependent wholly or in large part on the use of electronics."

Translation: No more paper, no more checks, no more cash. All of your chips will be silicon and locked inside a computer.

For reasons of convenience, efficiency, profitability, even safety, the banks and the Federal Reserve Board want to get rid of paper and the systems which use paper to transfer money or value. Whether EFT will get rid of paper is questionable. Even without the need for a check for payment, one expert estimates that with two purchases, one funds transfer, and one check deposit, the EFT system would still have to prepare and handle ten separate letters, notices, receipts, agreements, and statements.

In going paperless, in the drive toward the electronic valhalla, the financial-communications folk have put together two types of electronic systems to monitor and handle you and your money. One is called an "automated clearinghouse," which offers the bankers (and you?) two types of services. First, it can replace all of the checks and cash which you receive with electronic money in form of credits or blips or clicks or whistles. You and/or the bank can tell the ACH which accounts you want automatically and regularly paid (Ma Bell, Prudential, GMAC), and it will sort out those accounts and electronically credit them with your donation. That's why it's called an automated clearinghouse; it can automatically direct payments in many directions. There are dozens of these working right now in this country, some operated by private groups, but most run or controlled by the Federal Reserve Banks to handle trading between financial institutions. The biggest single push given these systems was provided by the Social Security Administration when it offered to distribute Social Security payment "value" this way. Many major corporations—IBM and Xerox among them—also use such systems to distribute payrolls to employees' bank accounts.

The other electronic system which makes Lifebank practical and workable is called the Transaction Card System. With this one, when you use your plastic card to buy something, that electronic terminal in the store will read your card, tell the computer how much you're spending, ask that that amount be either posted against your account or immediately deducted, and finally transfer the sum into the store's account. (It also gives the store instant updating on stock, inventory, sales, department performance, profit, and other essential facts.)

The combination of the automated clearing house and the transaction card system makes Lifebank not only practical and workable but also inevitable.

And it's all because of the bank cards.

One bank vice-president admitted, "A lot has been learned in processing credit cards that will be useful in electronic funds transfer systems. Preauthorized credit, card verification, and electronic interchange will all be necessary in electronic banking."

Another one, Bank of America's card expert Kenneth Larkin, said, "The credit card is on the leading edge in the field of electronic technology. Every draft that is negotiated by a Bank of America cardholder outside the state of California comes back to us in non-paper form. It comes back as electronic tape . . . Those occurring in the United States come back to us in a truly electronic funds transfer mode, and we are preparing to do this internationally."

One Philadelphia banker admits that 17% of all retail banking done at his place is "electronically driven."

Visa's president, Dee Hock, talking about branch banking for customer convenience, said, "Convenience will come to be electronic transfers."

Organizations made up of powerful financial institutions, corporations, and quasi-governmental groups have already been put together to organize and oversee these new systems. Membership includes not only the banks and holding companies which own the banks but also such highly involved bystanders as the Government Employees Credit Union, American Telephone and Telegraph Company, the Food Marketing Institute, General Electric Credit Corporation, the business-management firm of Price Waterhouse, and the U.S. Postal Service.

Today's slick, high-speed, sophisticated computers are so efficient that one despairing engineer commented, "They are capable of making a million mistakes a minute." Handling the job of isolating, identifying, sorting, cataloging, qualifying, and running the total financial affairs for this nation's 78 million bank card accounts is not only possible, but in a smaller way, is already being done. All the systems need are more terminals, more computers, more storage capacity, more communications lines to turn today's purchase-approving or transaction-transmitting and clearinghouse functions into the true Lifebank. Even back in the bank card's primitive days, machines which would be considered the Model T's of computers by today's standards could still whip out figures on the institution's bank card-program balance, what cardholders owed, what happened that day, an overall review of the card program, a list of purchase okays or authorizations, how merchant sales were going by different categories, details of card transactions that involved other banks, lost or stolen or fraudulent accounts, expired accounts, canceled-card lists, who was behind in paying, and who was overspending. They could do all of this without breathing hard, yet one engineer said, "They were electronic retards compared to today's whiz-kid generation of computers."

One Ohio bank was so sold on its computer's ability to sort, collate, differentiate, and handle millions of details in an orderly and profitable fashion that it issued not one or two, but five different cards to be used in machines. *The Journal of the American Bankers Association* called it ". . . the closest anyone has gotten so far to total electronic banking." That bank's electronics were asked to handle the myriad differences between the 150,000 regular BankAmericard accounts; 230,000 Bank 24 cards, which could be used in automated tellers; 35,000

ENTREE Cards for tellers, terminals, and check guarantee; 110,000 OK Cards, used to buy groceries and to cash Social Security or payroll checks; and the Share Account Card, used for purchases or drawing money by members of local credit unions.

Financial-communications systems have come a long way in a short time. Once, when you used your local bank card and approval was needed, the store clerk made a call, gave your number, and waited interminably while a bank clearance employee looked you up in a bulky stack of Rolodex cards. If that system were still in use, what you bought would be out of warranty before you even received approval to buy it. The heads of NBI (BankAmericard) and Interbank (Master Charge) realized that the only way an efficient and truly national bank card could work was with a high-speed national authorization system. That way, you could use your California-issued Bank-Americard in New York, your Illinois-issued Master Charge in Louisiana, and get approval before prices went up.

Putting together those first systems was not simple. For example, National BankAmericard officers met with twenty-one different companies including such giants as IBM, Burroughs, and TRW and gave them each over 21 pages of specifications for the system they wanted to build. Many of them, looking over the demands, passed. BASE (Bank-Americard Authorization System Experimental) I, a nationwide data-processing and communications system which tied together all of that organization's far-flung authorization centers, was started in August 1972 and was scheduled to begin giving the banks faster authorizations and around-the-clock service by April of the next year. In the meantime, the Interbank's Master Charge nationwide system was being assembled and had a start-up date of May 1 that year. Its assignment was to complete authorizations from anywhere in the country within one minute instead of the three to fifteen minutes it had taken before.

Demands on the systems exploded. In 1974, BASE I handled 6 million approvals or turndowns of credit. In the coming five years, Visa officials say that system must handle 1.25 billion a year—over 20,000% higher volume, all from the same system! The average response time, the time of getting your approval through, is now down to an incredible four seconds, even between some countries.

The foundation of Lifebank was being built, and the futurists of the industry could see it coming. In the National Bank-Americard Incorporated annual report for 1972, a section said, "The industry stands at the threshold of the era of electronic value exchange . . . Yet no new technology need be invented to achieve this potential . . . the technology exists and, indeed, is being applied." And later, "The list of today's BankAmericard activities and tomorrow's probabilities is almost limitless . . . If the bank card is to *evolve as a value exchange and identity device to meet the full financial needs of the consumers of the future,* new priorities must be established and much conceptual work completed. Organizational structures *to link the various existing technologies* will have to be created . . ." (Italics mine.)

Later, in 1978, Interbank's John Reynolds said, "We have to begin to reduce the amount of paper that is passing back and forth. Total EFT is really just around some future corner."

Just how future is that corner? The Bank of America undoubtedly believes it's at hand. In early 1980, that organization moved the executive in charge of the card program to a new spot, directly under the executive vice-president who heads B of A's electronic banking services. But the banks, savings and loan companies, credit unions, and mutual savings banks that will be involved in total EFT or Lifebank don't all agree. Some would like it to happen gradually, naturally, and inevitably. They point to the growth of bank cards as an example. First, bank cards were local, then regional, then finally national and international in recognition and services to carriers. At first, they were good for buying; then you could get a cash advance with them, transfer money, use them in place of checks. That's the way they believe EFT should happen. Today, a super-speedy way to okay your credit or pay for your purchases. Tomorrow, Lifebank?

Dale Browning of the Colorado National Bank once said, "There are many programs under way today that are moving with great speed to supply EFT services, or at least laying the foundation for EFT services. EFT, in my view, is progressing as it should progress; it's gradual, it's prudent, the services are well-thought-out, they're creating a reasonable environment for one experimentation, they're going from one phase into another phase, they're doing it without creating a lot of consumer confusion, they're *doing it with beginning acceptance, they're building credibility.*" (Italics mine.)

In other words, the go-slow bankers know that EFT and eventual Lifebank is not one of your greatest desires, and instead of dumping it all over you the way they did the bank cards, they are assembling it at a pace that won't panic people.

Many of them had read a *Harvard Business Review* special report on EFTS. That article reported that the governmental commission on EFTS had received many letters and petitions from citizens who were violently against the concept. "EFTS will invade privacy," "My money won't be safe," "Another example of jobs lost to technology," and "What are the real motives and intentions of the American financial community?" were some of the protests received. That report even added, "People have even likened EFTS to the book of Revelation's prediction of a 'Mark of the Beast,' the anti-Christ who would lead the world to destruction immediately preceding the second coming of Christ."

The bankers had probably also noticed a special study in a 1978 issue of *The Bankers Magazine* which looked into citizen reactions to EFT. Some 45% of the people asked disliked it somewhat or a great deal, while 25% liked it in some form. Another 29% were neutral, were waiting to see. Yet, close to 80% of all the people queried were using one or both bank cards, encouraging the bankers to go ahead with the systems. Along with other conclusions, *The Bankers Magazine* said, "Skepticism and distrust, or simple dislike, for the new systems are prevalent."

The all-seeing, all-knowing, all-controlling specter of Lifebank is more than enough reason for skepticism and distrust. But there are many other reasons EFT may be a time bomb they are building without reading the directions first.

1. EFT means computers, and computers do make mistakes. How many times have you tried to reason with or straighten out an unheeding, unresponsive, mistake-repeating computer? Some experts estimate that a computer can consistently make up to a 3% error. If that's true, and if 100 million of us were wired to an EFT system, it's possible that 3 million of us could

be incorrectly debited, classified, cataloged, or even deprived totally of any buying power. More importantly, all of your value could be in one file. Today, if one department-store computer fouls up your account, you can still shop at other stores while trying (usually in vain) to straighten out the mess. With one central file, with only one computer system involved, an error against you could literally wipe out your ability to buy shelter, clothing, food, transportation, and other life-sustaining essentials.

2. Even if the computer lets you live, it could be at a high price. Investigators have found that some of today's "accurate" computers seem to have been programmed by a loan shark. There are many ways credit-card computers can cheat you. These are some of them:

> Sending you a bill without giving you credit for payments.

> Making out your bill but not sending it to you, so you'll owe interest later.

> Not telling you if you overpaid and then keeping the extra money.

> Telling you when you made a mistake but not telling you when it does.

> Rounding off numbers, always at your expense.

> Creating extra charges which just happen to equal the amount of credit you might have coming back.

Commenting on these "accidents," one publication reported that these thefts or deceptions were justified by management as accepted business practices, that dishonesty of the customer was higher than dishonesty of the business, and even that the system was perfect as long as it met management's goals.

3. If you know what you're doing, it is easier to rob a computer than an unprotected liquor store. And the rewards are considerably greater.

119

A liquor-store holdup might net you $500. An FBI study reported in the Los Angeles *Times* says that embezzlers steal an average of $19,000. Yet, the average theft from on-line computer systems is $450,000! The people who tap these golden tills are an ingenious lot. Some program the system to increase their own salaries or to get extra payroll checks, Social Security payments, or tax refunds. They also program that same computer to forget those payments once they're made, so there's no recoverable trace of those thefts. Others program computers to give good credit ratings to people who are bad risks. These new ratings are then either used by gangs to go out and loot stores with new cards or are sold profitably to people who need them. Several firms that advertise "bad-credit-cleared-up" services in the classified advertisements of the newspapers have used inside technicians to reverse client credit ratings. Still other sly operators program the computer to deliver payroll checks to them two, three, or more years after they have quit the company and have been forgotten. One high school student even used a computer to break its own security code. And another thief used a computer to find out how much he could steal before the computer issued an alarm. Finding out the figure, he kept his robbery below that level.

Most studies show that computer crime is committed mainly by the people who build or operate the systems. If they can dream it up or make it work for major corporations, they can also make it work for themselves. Too, most computer manipulators are young and have never been in trouble, so they have no criminal record to forewarn the companies. The computer-dependent organizations like Visa and MasterCard are purely at the mercy of these people. Even if they suspect an employee of tampering with the electronic books, most companies will merely fire the person but will not go to the expense of making changes in the computer's security system. That way, the fired employee can just as easily help himself from outside as he could when working within.

To combat this, there are new and sophisticated security devices being installed in the systems. IBM has one which scrambles messages so an outsider can't decode them (but someone who works with the computer or someone who designed the system can). Another company builds in different levels of security for different levels of employees (but it's breakable by certain employees and technicians). Special codes are also passed out to programmers and operators so the computer can recognize how cleared the person is or whether that person is allowed to tamper with the machine. According to the Los Angeles *Times*, the Japanese have come up with a special lip-print reader, which identifies people who can use the computer, but according to reports, employees are turned off by kissing a computer before they can turn it on.

All of the losses experienced by the bank card companies through counterfeit cards, stolen and lost cards, merchant crooks, and fraud will look like petty cash as more and more of your value gets put into computer banks and more and more dishonest computer brains rob those banks, sometimes merely by making a telephone call.

And, just as you are now indirectly charged to make up those existing fraud losses, you'll be indirectly assessed to reimburse the banks for those future ones. Despite the banks' "shuffling" of figures (which always comes out lower), total losses through fraud are running over $1 billion a year, according to some observers. With the total EFT system, with each till-tapping running an average of, say, $500,000, those losses could run into multibillions and you will pay for them or the banks will go belly-up, leaving you in an even deeper hole.

4. Today, you have many cards: Visa, MasterCard, Sears, Texaco, Standard Oil, department stores. With EFT you could have one "financial" or Lifebank card. Today, if you lose a Visa or it is stolen, the misuse of that card is limited to $50 even if you don't notify the bank-card company in time. And you still have the other cards on which you can live. Even if you weren't protected by a law which limits your loss to $50, that loss is limited to the credit on that one card. When you have one Lifebank card and it is lost or stolen, all of your savings, financial equities, investments, value of every kind that you own, could be in jeopardy, could be tapped for withdrawal or crediting to another account. Smart computer manhandlers could easily use your lost or stolen card to drain your accounts and then even program the computer to "forget" where your money went. You would be stone broke. The thief would be instantly wealthier. There would be absolutely no trail or way

to trace the crime. Some of the nation's prisons might even be helping these perfect crimes to come about. They are offering convicted embezzlers, thieves, and others courses in computer programming.

5. EFT not only opens spectacular new possibilities for money crimes but can make possible theft of whatever privacy you have left. Today, facts about you are scattered around. Your schools have some, the armed forces may have others, the Social Security people, the Internal Revenue Service, the department store credit sections, the credit card companies, all have bits and pieces of information about you. With EFT and Lifebank, all of that information would be collected automatically in a "cumulative record." Where your money comes from, your physical condition and medical history, how you spend your money, how you vote, where and if you worship, how you travel and where you entertain, what you buy, whom you live with, when and why you've been in trouble, how much you drink or whether you use drugs—all of that and much more would be included in a continually updated profile and biography of you. This would happen when all of the private and governmental computers were tied together. When asked about you, by name or number, each would contribute its tidbits of information and gossip until that complete master file was assembled. Too much detail for one file? Not to worry. One communications-machinery supplier was given the assignment to come up with a computer tape that could record twelve pages of information on a person. If more is needed, more page capacity can be added.

Right now, these records are considered the property of the people who have them—government agencies, banks, credit bureaus, credit card companies, insurance companies, other institutions. Although they are about you, they are not yours, you do not own them, even though it is a seizure of personal papers. That's what the courts say. What that means is that you really have no legal right to decide who can see them. Too, there is no cutoff date on how long those pieces of information stay in the file. What you did as a wayward youth can stay there forever. The one time you went into hock and couldn't make your payments will be there to see for anyone who can get access to your file. Professor Alan Westin, appearing before the National Commission on EFTS, said your file should be "valuable legal property belonging only to the individual account holder and not to the system." But the way things are today, the system owns them.

With all of the inside details of your life hanging bare in that file, you are going to be a sitting duck for anyone who wants a handout. First in line will be the biggest open palm, the federal government. The IRS could demand and get complete access to your Lifebank information. At first it would be to check your tax return or to run an audit. Later, it could use the computers to do your entire return and deduct and transfer what you owe, all automatically. Court orders for parking tickets, for alimony, for fines, could be electronically deducted when filed against you. If you are on welfare or unemployment, your file could be checked to make sure you have no other income, and your welfare income might even be coded so it could be spent only for bread and never for beer.

The police and investigative organizations could use those files to get evidence, to find crime, to track fugitives, and to locate them. One idea even suggests that paroled prisoners would be given a card which could be used only in a certain area. If the prisoner left that area, he or she would not have credit or spending power for food, for clothing, for shelter. Another possible but farfetched plan would even control geographical population imbalance by limiting how many cards could be used in a city, a county, a state. If the controllers wanted Iowa more populated and California less, making survival possible only in Iowa could encourage tens of thousands to move there.

All of these controls are possible. Some will not happen because you and millions like you will demand new laws, new regulations, which will give you protection from certain invasions of your privacy and certain losses of liberty. But there will be lobbying and plea-bargaining and compromises, and the overall result will be a continuing erosion of your privacy. The police will probably not get total freedom to investigate and monitor your file and will have to show "just cause" to do it, just like getting a search warrant today. Getting a search warrant for the police these days is not that difficult.

The government may not be able to tap your account for

taxes they feel due without a hearing of some type. But you know how many taxpayers come out ahead on IRS hearings. The great danger will not even be the legal access to your Lifebank account, but unauthorized entry. A computer-trained cop, a systems-oriented IRS employee, a private detective, a blackmailer, will be able to sit down at a mini-computer and punch up your entire life in a matter of seconds. Those queries and investigations won't be traceable, either, because your file computer will be instructed to deliver the information like a good little boy, and then forget it ever happened. Most of this will be done in the name of protection—for the government, for the financial system, for our streets and neighborhoods, and for lucky you.

Some bankers and card companies are making all of this easier, more practical, and more possible by working to develop one code which can be read and transmitted in all of the electronic communications systems throughout the world. In looking for an easy solution to simplify "reading" of cards in different types of terminals, in different types of computer systems, even in different countries, those bankers would like one universal magnetic code used for everything. That code plus many details about you and your card would be included on that dark stripe on the back of your bank card, would be an integral part of your eventual Lifebank card.

You will become your financial or Lifebank card. One report says that the government has definite plans to catalog everyone and to verify identities. Methods for identifying you will be designed to work with EFT. Some of the ideas being forwarded are fingerprint recognition by the computer, voice recognition, natural electric signals from your body, handprints; even a personalized miniature transmitter which could be implanted into your body to give off a distinctive signal is being considered. These systems, which would replace a plastic card, answer the cliché questions about paying tolls, losing cards, or where to carry a Lifebank in a bikini. One New York CPA has even come up with the solution for corporate identity. His answer: have the corporate treasurer use his right thumb for personal identification, his left one for company business.

What you will definitely get or already have is called a PIN. That Personal Idenification Number is already being used by some bank card carriers to get cash advances and to conduct other transactions. PINs, excuse the expression, are sticky. There are too many ways others can get your PIN and use it to tap your account for money, for information, or both. In making up lists of PINs for people, magnetic tape is used. That tape can be duplicated, stolen, or questioned electronically for the material on it. Too, whenever that PIN is used on paper, that paper could be examined by unauthorized people. Today, with your PIN, thieves can get into automatic-teller machines and use your number in stores. Tomorrow, they will be able to get into Lifebank. The basic trouble with PIN is that it only tells the machine that the card is good, it does not tell the machine if the person using the card is.

A governmental official, Virginia H. Knauer, once warned the Commission, "EFTS opens both the consumer and financial institutions to a whole new dimension of fraud—fraud through computer theft. Persons who gain electronic access to an EFT system can steal not only money but also data on consumers."

Today, more than 98% of all large banks offer or plan to offer their customers automated services. So they have the machinery. The two bank card systems certainly have developed worldwide communications systems to the state of the art. If you have a credit card of any type, especially a bank card, you are already cross-indexed, cataloged, profiled, and put in your place in a computer bank. There are automated clearinghouses and computer centers and thousands of miles of dedicated telephone lines tying them all together. There are thousands of point-of-sale and transaction terminals already in place at airports, in shopping malls, on street corners, on campuses. Everything is ready to go. So what's the holdup? Why isn't Lifebank here already?

There are basically three things delaying it. The high cost of putting a complete and total Lifebank operation into action is one. Selling the idea to us is the second. Attracting unfavorable legislation that could cut down freedom of operations and profits is the third. For those reasons, some bankers and financial experts are suddenly reversing themselves, taking a second look at how Lifebank might go together.

Visa's Dee Hock, who is recognized as one of the longtime backers of "electronic exchange of value," surprised just about everyone in late 1977 when he said, "[EFT] is a figment of the imagination. No such system has or ever will exist. We are merely experiencing an accelerating evolution in the exchange of value, whereby the processing and transportation of alpha/numeric value messages is done on electronic impulse rather than on paper."

That probably came as a surprise to *Fortune* magazine, which printed, "The nation needs a consumer EFT system, and it will eventually get one. . . . A fully developed EFT system will contribute to a more efficient allocation of the nation's resources. Those who argue that we may not need EFT fail to grasp its ultimate significance."

Two years after Hock's statement, above, Visa's marketing director, Philip Hayman, begged to disagree with his boss, when he said to a group of bankers, "The volume of transactions has become so enormous that transfer by means of an electronic pulse at the rate of thousands of bits per second is the new necessity, the new system for the worldwide exchange of value."

Other bankers are also quarreling among themselves. In fact, at bank card conventions the third-most-popular topic is EFT. (The two most-popular topics perennially remain how to make more money and how to get the government off of the banks' back.)

One estimate says that the banks have already invested over $6 billion in electronic equipment but that they would probably need another $12 billion or more to put together a total and complete EFT system, the kind which Lifebank demands.

One of those automatic cash dispensers costs about $20,000 and roughly $5,000 a year to operate. Those humanless automatic tellers run $40,000 and about $10,000 a year to run. Terminals, switches, and communications wires aren't cheap, either, except that the telephone company, as a monopoly, is supposed to offer maximum efficiency at lowest price for those. New techniques, however, show that computers can be linked by radio or infrared waves, if telephone-line costs get too high.

To many bankers, EFT is a service we can all use but only a few would pay for. Banks are profit-making organizations, and they know that you wouldn't be too thrilled to get a bill for your share of the EFT machinery they wanted to buy. They're stuck with paying for it all, at least at first. Most banks already have large amounts of money tied up in expensive check-processing equipment. If they add massive electronics, they are paying for two value-exchange systems.

The answer is volume. One of the members of that national EFT commission estimated that if a large bank or group of them put out 3–5,000 terminals and each one handled 5,000 pieces of business a month, the costs of each transaction would be less than a nickel, or much less than the cost of processing a check. A bank-card publication recently pointed out that bankers are beginning to realize this and that there would be a 50% growth in automatic tellers this year and another 50% next year and some 246,000 of them in place worldwide by 1985.

Although generally pleading poverty, most of the large banks can definitely afford to invest in EFT. The Los Angeles *Times* reported: California's Security Pacific turned up with record earnings of $164.5 million for 1979; that same state's Wells Fargo & Co. admitted it netted $130.2 million for that year; New York's Manufacturers Hanover made $211.3 million; and Pittsburgh's Mellon ended the year $101 million to the good. The story was the same pretty much throughout the country. And the newly introduced card fees and higher interest rates will increase bank profits dramatically. When they decide to go ahead full steam, the money is there.

The next problem which concerns bankers is possible legislation against a total EFT or Lifebank system. They know that congressional committees and subcommittees which watch things financial are very sensitive to public reaction. They also know that there is already some hostility out there in the real world about "losing my money to a machine," "invasion of my privacy," and "trying to deal with computers." There is also the problem of branch banking. A federal act, which may be revised soon, says that no bank can put branches outside of its home state. In addition, dozens of those home states also either limit branch banking or prohibit it altogether within the state. That brings up the problem of automatic tellers. Is an unattended, completely electronic-mechanical device a branch office of a bank? It can take deposits, transfer money from one account to another, deliver cash, and provide other banking services. Is the fact that no one's home reason enough to disqualify it as a branch? Or is it a triumph of technology over law? There are many trial cases going on around the country to test this question. Illinois, Colorado, Minnesota, and Missouri are some of the states which have said those automatic tellers are branch banks and are illegal. If they are, then the EFT system which needs terminals to work is going to be slowed down while the bank lobbyists get to work trying to change those laws.

The easiest way to change them is to get public pressure on the banks' side. Even if it's not best in the long run, if voters want something, they get it (look at some of our politicians). And getting the vote from the voters is a job for the bank marketing people, the money motivators.

They know, the advertising and marketing people do, that trying to sell you the answer to a problem you don't recognize is a tough task. An old motto says, "If it isn't broken, why repair it?" Most people feel that the present checks/currency/credit-card system may be breaking them, but certainly isn't broken itself.

The past dozen or so years in which EFT has been developed have seen the human, electronic, and mechanical pieces fit together. During those years, hardly anyone in banking thought about *selling* the system to us. It was computers, not commercials; automation instead of advertising; electronic billing instead of electric billboards. The operations departments of the card companies and banks did their jobs so well that technology passed need, and that need must be created.

Now comes the hard sell. For the next several years you will be increasingly assaulted by advertising and publicity barrages designed to convince you that pulp paper is bad, that electronic impulses are the good guys. The message will come from the banks, from the credit-card companies, and from the stores. Their combined advertising budgets will run into hundreds of millions a year. You will be told and sold on the many advantages of electronic banking: 24-hour-a-day access to your "value" from anywhere in the world; street-corner automatic-teller convenience; no more unbalanced checkbooks; new safety for your money; two years' buying power in your pocket; and dozens more carefully researched appeals designed to motivate you toward EFT.

There will also be "promotions," giveaways of one type or

another to get you to sit on the table and eat off the chair. To help you forget about loss of control of your money, about error-ridden computers, about invasions of your privacy, you will get the financial version of a new toaster or TV set. To encourage initial use, you could be offered a bank or store discount, say, a 2% savings on everything you buy through the EFT system, or maybe $10 a month in additional credits if your payroll check is automatically put into your Lifebank and authorized payments are taken out. Worried about losing your "float," the time it takes for a check you write to reach the bank and be processed? Many people are. They use that time to scrape up the cash to cover that check. Or, how about not being able to put a stop on a check when you get a bad deal? The bank merchandisers will come up with a plan which proves they're saving money for you if you'll switch from those bothersome checks to EFT or Lifebank. They will also increase check charges and lower EFT charges, so electronics will be the economic way for you to go. When you do, you will probably get a new waffle iron, too.

They will even try to humanize the whirring, clicking, roboted industry. First National Bank of Atlanta did it by painting their automatic tellers a warm red-and-yellow combination and advertising them as your chum, "Tillie the Alltime Teller."

Once you're in the system, of course, things will change. You will become more and more dependent upon your lifeline to Lifebank as the bankers squeeze out the checking system, close down the currency possibilities, and push you more and more toward the elastic plastic that will do everything.

Even if some credit and bank card people are saying that there will be no EFT, no eventual Lifebank, should you listen to them?

In 1979, Dee Hock prepared a speech for bankers in which he wrote:

"There are several fundamental convictions which underlie Visa's activities.

"First: There is one thing common to all mankind. The need to exchange value. To exchange what one owns, or can reasonably expect to earn, for that which is needed and desired.

"Second: The primary function of the financial services

129

industry is to provide the most reliable, least expensive means by which that may be done.

"Third: The exchange of value goes far beyond the transfer of funds and payment systems. It includes the standards, technology and methods by which electronics are applied to payroll, retailing, and communications.

"Fourth: There is an irrevocable, constantly growing need for a worldwide method for the exchange of value which transcends nations, regions, language, economic practice, and political belief.

"Fifth: Exchange of value in the future will be primarily electronic and done by those most skilled in the electronic manipulation of data and telecommunications. . . ."

. . . and us?

8

Laying Down the Law

"IF WE HAD less legislation and more questions being asked by politicians of consumers as to what they really want—not just the few fanatics who have complaints or the few legitimate people who have complaints, but asked of the tens of thousands and the millions—you would find out that people love the bank credit card . . ." That was part of a statement made in 1977 by Kenneth Larkin, Bank of America's combination bank card pioneer and man of the financial future.

If it is true, as Larkin believes, that people do love their bank cards now, then it is precisely the efforts of the politicians and the passing of demanded legislation which made these cards into heart's desire.

Consider how lovable the bank card was back in the early 1970's. Let's say you had a card from a bank that was really out for your buck and its motto was "Let the bearer beware." (Not all banks used these tactics, but enough did to bring on thundering public resentment and a Congress that snapped to.)

First, your bank changed the calendar. They tidied up our traditional messy one by organizing the year into twelve thirty-day months. That gave them five extra days a year to charge you extra interest.

The billing people there deliberately delayed mailing out

your monthly bill. When you got it, your "free" period was cut down so badly you couldn't get payment back in time to cut off those extra finance charges.

Because you were overcharged for a lawn mower you bought two months ago, you were mad, didn't use the card last month. That's okay with the bank. They billed you a finance or service charge on the overcharge anyway.

They took their own sweet time looking into that lawn mower overcharge you refused to pay. Included in a new billing were costs for their investigation, a charge for the duplicate sales slip they enclosed, and a 15% "attorney's fee" because you were delinquent and hadn't paid for the lawn mower.

They had also changed your credit rating from good to bad and showed it to anyone who wanted to see it.

They demanded payment now, and if you were still unhappy with the error, they said they were going to take the money out of your checking or savings account to pay that bill.

So you paid, hoping to clear it up later. Although it took one day for your check to get to the bank, they didn't credit you with that payment for another week. That way they could charge more interest.

You even deliberately overpaid a few dollars to make sure all of their charges were covered. When they got that extra money, you weren't credited with it.

After all, the bank finally pointed out, they weren't responsible for the lawn mower. They lent you the money to buy, that's all. If you had a complaint with that grass cutter, your beef was with the store. Since the store had already been paid for that tool by the bank, the chances of getting your money back were the same as they are in a Las Vegas casino.

But you considered yourself lucky anyway. After all, you had one of those new hard-wearing, waterproof passports to prosperity—a bank card. Look at the hundreds of thousands who couldn't get one: women, blacks, Hispanics, senior citizens, people who lived in certain neighborhoods, who worked at certain jobs, who had limited incomes—they were turned down by the banks and never even told why.

Those were just some of the free-rolling, extra-money-making, highhanded tactics many banks were using.

There were more.

Representative Frank Annunzio, the tough, consumer-guarding Illinois Democrat who headed the House Consumer Affairs subcommittee, said, "We are getting more complaints on credit cards than from any other consumer area." And *Business Week* magazine reported that "Congress wants to know why the credit card industry draws so many complaints."

Many complaints were about that indecipherable language known as "Bankerspeak." Examples of it usually appeared on bank card agreements and statements, were set in head-of-a-needle-size type, and printed in some obscure location. John Quinn, director of Maine's Bureau of Consumer Protection, once presented an example of this, taken directly from a credit card disclosure notice.

It said, "The Finance Charge balance will not include the average daily balance of purchases previously billed or posted during the billing period if Holder has paid Holder's previous balance in full within 20 days from the previous billing date or if Holder's previous balance was zero or a credit balance."

As they say in pool halls, run that by me again, Charley. Notice that there are four different mentions of four different balances sprinkled throughout the sentence, which "quite effectively eliminated any possibility that its customers might perceive what the bank actually intended to accomplish." Quinn added, ". . . the bank was careful to avoid any possibility that its customers might somehow understand the new system."

Another banker, speaking at a convention, boasted that his organization sent out a notice so "cleverly written" that even attorneys were calling to ask what it meant.

Other loud complaints were coming into Washington about the banks' creative interest structures. With no industry-wide standards for charging interest and with freedom to charge that interest in various ways, each bank could come up with a way of figuring it which made the most money. With different methods for counting what you owed, how much you had paid, and the time intervals involved, you could be socked 50% or more difference in interest rates from one bank to another.

Congress took its first look at bank credit cards in 1967; it was concentrating on the mass-mailing mess that had made some of the nation's, and especially Chicago's, thieves as rich as banks. As the years had gone by, as tens of millions of cards began to be slapped down on restaurant tables, store counters, and repair-shop desks, card carrier complaints increased by the hundreds and the need for controls became increasingly more evident.

In the late 1960's, the first important legislation was passed to protect you from some of the bank-card abuses. Known as the Truth-in-Lending Act, this law said that the banks had to tell what you were paying in annual interest rates, total dollar costs, and finance charges, along with any other costs of credit. It also told the credit card companies that they could no longer mail out cards unless people asked for them; that if a card was lost or stolen, card carrier liability was limited to $50; and it limited how much of salary or income could be grabbed from anyone to pay debts.

Later, the unsolicited-card portion of that law was cleverly bypassed by some bankers who hired "marketing" companies to telephone people and ask if they wanted a bank card. During a special hearing, Representative Annunzio found out that these telephone solicitors were paid by their performance and would tell the banks to send cards to people who hadn't agreed to receive one. Some of these pitches were disguised as surveys. The caller would ask, "Would you use a credit card if you had one?" If the person on the other end of the line said, "Sure," one was mailed, and another bank-card carrier had been recruited.

The Truth-in-Lending Act headed a decade of legislative moves constructed to protect you and other bank card users from the freeform, self-serving policies of the banks. It also began ten years of intense examination of consumer rights versus bank rights, by economists, congressmen, educators, attorneys, judges, juries, and courts. They were all trampling around in a new legal swamp, with no visible footprints to guide them. Bank cards were a new phenomenon, and the impact and effect on us and our society had never been expected, so there were no existing laws to handle the problems. As Annunzio's chief of staff, Curtis Prins, said, "We never had a credit card economy before, so we didn't know what would happen."

134

In fact, so little was understood about the impact of cards in those early days that an Iowa judge dismissed a person accused of having a stolen credit card. The judge maintained that the card itself was of no value, and besides, Iowa had no law at the time against having a stolen card.

In 1971, the Fair Credit Reporting Act was passed. It said that credit information about you should be fair and accurate; that you had the right to know what was in your credit file and to fix any mistakes in it; that your file could only be used certain ways; and that if you were turned down for credit you could find out who gave you a bad report and why. Things were looking up.

More laws were passed; some mentioned changes in the credit business on riders or amendments or portions of other bills. One was the Fair Credit Billing Act of 1974. Included in this law was a section which finally said you could deduct the price of something you wanted to return from your bill, until the dispute was straightened out, without the bank giving you forty financial lashes. To avoid nickel-and-diming them to death, bank lobbyists got the bill compromised so that the purchase had to be for more than $50 and made within 100 miles of the place the bank sent your bill.

One of the most bitterly contested pieces of legislation was the 1976 Equal Credit Opportunity Act. With that, the law said you couldn't be turned down for a bank card or credit because of your sex, marital status, race, color, religion, national origin, age, or even because your money came from welfare or public-assistance programs. The banks couldn't even refuse if you were a "troublemaker" and constantly demanded your rights under other laws. If you were turned down, you had to be told why within thirty days. Other important parts of that law decided that if both husband and wife qualified for cards separately, they could have individual accounts; that your mate didn't have to sign for you; that those accounts had to be handled in both names if you wanted it that way; and that the bank couldn't call in your card because later you were divorced or married, changed your name, or retired.

The law still rankles most bankers. B of A's Larkin had a great deal to say about that type of legislation during a special discussion held by a group of bankers:

"The end result [of legislation and regulations] could well be that another 'right' will be added to the fundamental rights of the American citizen, and that 'right' will be the right to credit. We have not considered that a 'right' up to this moment; we've considered it something he gets if he warrants it."

Later in that same series of comments, he added, ". . . to the extent that this goes on, week after week, and month after month, the parameters for our expressing credit judgments just get more and more confined, to the point where, if a prospective borrower comes in and he's breathing and he can sign his name on the note, you must by law give credit to him."

In 1978, the Financial Institutions Regulatory and Interest Rate Control Act gave you the right to financial privacy from federal-government peekers. If an agency of the government wanted to see your credit files, they had to tell you about it, and you could challenge that curiosity.

All of this regulation didn't sit too well with the banks. Not only did it tell them what they couldn't do, but it required more people, more paperwork, more time from everybody's schedule to change the already-set-up systems. They believed that this policing of their practices was costing them and you too much money. Joseph J. Pinola, chairman of the board of Western Bancorporation, said in 1979, "Regulation is costing America well over $100 billion a year—and rising. It is a major contributor to inflation."

Through the years, as the bank cards grew increasingly powerful, so did laws covering problems that card users were discovering in the systems. Throughout the nation, people and groups were climbing on the sue-the-bank wagon.

In 1974 a BankAmericard carrier from Sacramento, California, filed a $20 million class-action suit against Bank of America, basically saying that the late charges on his billing were purely arbitrary and that there was no relationship between those charges and any damages suffered by the bank. The bank countered by saying the charges were fair.

That same year, Consumers Union, the nonprofit outfit that publishes *Consumer Reports*, charged BankAmericard and American Express with violating antitrust laws. Consumers Union felt that merchants should have the option to offer discounts to people who bought for cash, because credit card sales cost the merchant more due to the bank kickback. It was, according to them, "illegal price fixing and a restraint of trade." The executive director of CU at the time said that both card companies' agreements with merchants said they couldn't give a better price to cash customers. BankAmericard's head lawyer denied the allegation by answering that their contracts did not include pricing requirements, that each bank had its own contract with the stores, and it was up to those banks to obey the law.

The strangest, most significant lawsuit filed during the 1970's was what one executive called "the worthless Worthen case." For a while, it looked as if it might wreck the bank-card business by attracting government trust-busters to go in and disassemble that industry. When all the pointing-with-alarm was over, however, the lawsuit actually created the gold-town boom which swept the bank card into today's all-powerful position.

It is known as the "duality" case, and is covered in other chapters. But what happened there is one of the main reasons we are at this frightening stage. It is a story worth twice-telling.

Basically, what happened is that a small financial institution called Worthen Bank & Trust Company of Little Rock, Arkansas, filed a suit saying that National BankAmericard Incorporated (BankAmericard administrative headquarters) was violating the Sherman Antitrust Act. That bank complained about a bylaw in NBI's agreement with its banks. The bylaw said BankAmericard "A" banks (the major ones) could not also have a Master Charge program in the same bank. Worthen had signed up with the Master Charge system before that bylaw was passed. They claimed to have lost a great deal of money during the Christmas season because that bylaw prevented the bank from starting its Master Charge program. Their attorney wanted triple damages for the Christmas profits they had lost, plus a court order keeping NBI from banning "dual" membership.

One of NBI's executives reported that "Hock was in shock." Dee Hock had always been a great verbalizer about the advantages of free enterprise and competition as the True Way.

He saw this lawsuit as a threat to everything red, white, and blue as well as everything blue, white, and gold, the colors of his card. If single banks could issue both cards, then in Hock's opinion there was no competition between BankAmericard and Master Charge. It could eventually become one system and the government would call it a monopoly and try to regulate it, he feared.

The attorney for Worthen didn't see it that way, said that NBI's stance actually kept competition down by not allowing individual banks to issue both cards so they could compete with other banks.

On July 20, 1972, Judge Miller of a U.S. District Court in Arkansas came up with a summary judgment which said, roughly, that NBI was in violation of antitrust laws and that it couldn't stop its banks from handing out both cards.

That wasn't the end of it.

Restraining orders, preliminary injunctions, stipulations, interrogatories, access to records, motions, appeals, and all those other weapons of legal warfare were brandished and used by one or both sides. Finally somebody said, "I'll take this all the way to the Supreme Court." And they did.

But the Supreme Court, not wanting to get involved, sent it back to the Little Rock federal court for a full trial. After some five years of to-ing and fro-ing, and trying to avoid a trial, NBI finally gave in and reluctantly said their banks could also handle Master Charge programs.

Suddenly banks were no longer exclusively Visa- or Master Charge-handling organizations. People who had Visa from one bank and Master Charge from another found themselves with both cards from both banks, plus additional cards from banks across town, upstate, or out of the area. By giving each bank the possibility of doubling its number of card carriers and the amount of money they could spend, the bank card business was headed for the sky. But that same sky was falling for the increasingly antiquated idea of saving up until you could afford something and keeping a balanced budget at home.

Dee Hock could not believe the outcome. By keeping the systems apart, Hock felt there was fair competition and that the antitrust people couldn't move against the bank card systems.

Instead, the courts and agencies saw it the other way, said that he was keeping the individual banks from competing. There is continuing fear at Visa, and to some extent at MasterCard, that the end of this is not yet in sight.

The subject will undoubtedly come up again. The lawmakers could get involved. In that case, it is possible that Visa and MasterCard would be considered one and could eventually be put under federal utility regulation, like AT&T. "Why not do it that way?" observed one disgruntled card carrier jokingly. "I get wrong numbers from both of them anyway."

Another solution could be the individual bank's desire to cut operational costs by eliminating one of the systems. Currently, here and there across the country, customers or card administrators are being asked to choose either Visa or MasterCard by bank management which then drops the loser.

While attention was concentrated on other problems, the fantasy of electric money was becoming a reality. The wiring up of the bank card business was well under way. The card people were letting the silicon chips fall where they may. Electronic cash registers were popping up all over stores, automated tellers were growing on street corners, cash machines were holding up walls. And they were all connected to switches or computers or other systems which silently, relentlessly hummed onward, continuously capturing financial data and our economic system, all at the same time.

That Champion of the Card Carrier, Frank Annunzio, got things stirred up again. In December 1977 he held the first of a series of field hearings, this one in Chicago. Other legislators there included Wylie from Ohio, Fary of Chicago, La Falce from New York, Vento from Minnesota. Although other credit card problems were studied, the most concentrated attention went to electronic funds transfer. Annunzio pointed out that consumers didn't seem to want electronic banking. He said that Texas had held a referendum on whether EFTS should be allowed in that state and voters turned it down, two-to-one. In addition, a large California savings-and-loan organization had discontinued a multimillion-dollar EFTS program and the largest bank in Iowa had stopped a five-month test of EFTS because its customers didn't use it very much. What concerned him was that the banking industry was moving doggedly ahead with these systems. ". . . financial institutions are not going to spend millions of dollars on EFTS equipment and then leave it up to consumer whim as to whether or not the system will be used. There may well be an attempt to force consumers to use EFTS and that is why the safeguards contained in this bill are so vitally needed. EFTS has been described as . . . .'King Kong in search of a trainer,'" he added.

Annunzio was ready with whip and chair.

In a hearing a few months later, he made three "charges":

". . . I would like to charge that instead of developing a strategy for plastic-card operations, banks have virtually leaped first and then looked to see where they might land.

". . . I would further like to charge that EFTS and the Edsel have a lot in common—something which looks good on paper but simply will not sell. I am not convinced that the large scale development of such systems is presently in the interests of the country, the banks or the public.

"I find the talk of a universal all-purpose card a bit frightening. If I were to receive a card tomorrow which would allow merchants to access my checking account, permit withdrawals at cash machines, and an automatic line of credit, I would do only one thing—cut the card up into twenty-five little pieces and send it back to the bank."

Annunzio admitted he had played a trick on his audience. Those "charges" had actually not been made by Annunzio, but by financial men. The first had been issued by John S. Reed, executive vice-president of New York's Citibank. The second was made by Keith W. Hughes, vice-president of San Francisco's Crocker Bank. And the third statement was offered by Robert E. Knight, an economist with the Federal Reserve Bank of Kansas City.

Then Annunzio began cracking that whip. "I find it very difficult," he said, "to understand why those who promote electronic funds transfer systems are unwilling to endorse even the most basic consumer safeguards. It is that 'consumer be damned' attitude that led to the drafting of this legislation . . ."

He pointed out that so much money was being spent on EFTS that financial institutions would start forcing people to use it and then charge them for that use. As evidence, he listed a practice in Syracuse, New York, in which people who wanted to pay by check instead of by electronic machine were charged $3.00 extra. Another banking organization charged 25¢ each time a person took cash from an automatic dispenser. There was other evidence, too.

The legislation he put into the congressional mill had several hard-hitting areas aimed straight at electronic money systems. His original bill had sections saying the banks couldn't falsely advertise EFT services; couldn't charge more if you paid by check than by EFT card; that you could stop payment (like stopping a check) when you used that card; that you were responsible for only $50 loss if your EFT card was lost or stolen; and, among other protections, that you would get a printed or written receipt whenever you used the nontraceable electronic pathways. It also had a strongly worded area which kept the banks from demanding that you use the EFT system. Without that section, for example, the banks could easily turn down a loan request unless you agreed to pay it back through the electric animal.

After many considerations, concurrences, suggested amendments, changes, adjustments, deletions, rewordings, and compromises, a version of the EFT bill was passed by Congress and went into working law early in 1980. Most of the EFT-beast training had shaped it up, but some key issues didn't get through. The bank lobbyists worked long and hard hours to keep the originally suggested legislation from pulling the plug on their existing electronic lashups. One important section was bitterly disputed, finally ended up on the congressional cutting room floor. What you lost in that scissoring was the right to stop payment on a purchase when you used a "financial transaction" card. In that way, electronic card buying was like purchasing with cash. If your purchase didn't work out, you had to go fight the merchant to get satisfaction. It was definitely not like paying by check, which you could stop until you and the store worked out some settlement.

There were other deletions, changes, and modifications too, but we finally had a law that could slow down but not stop the momentum of Lifebank.

For years now the bankers have been defending electronic development as a logical, sane, and practical way to go. For them. For us. They feel that the electronic wiring of the economy will save you money because it will cost less to handle your banking and buying; that you will be able to get to your money twenty-four hours a day anywhere in the world; that the problems with stolen or forged or misused checks will disappear. Doing business with an electronic card, one pointed out, is a great deal easier than having to write out a check, enter the check details on a stub, wait for a clerk to write down driver's license and credit card numbers, and have a manager come by to initial that check.

Another one said, "Consumers . . . don't really care whether they use a piece of plastic or a piece of paper. They don't care whether that payment is electronically handled or whether it's a paper-based transaction."

Since the electronic "debit" card replaces checks and immediately deducts what you spend from what you have, other bankers were worried that you would resent giving up your "float." That's the free period it takes the check to get to the bank, or the increasingly shorter period you get from billing time to paying time with your bank card. All agreed that those floats cost the banks money; and those costs were being indirectly passed on to you. One important banker even said, "The credit card free period really has been a gift . . . for years. It is inevitable that before too long we will see widespread charges for cards." That prediction came true in mid-1980.

Bankers were also pretty well agreed that national (and international) electronic webs would contain our money in the future. What they disagreed on was how long it would take and how complex the system would be. Visa's Charles Russell said to other bankers, ". . . when your marketplace is wired and you reach the point where you can risk giving everyone with whom you deal some type of a transaction card, and every other marketplace in the country is similarly wired, you can then afford to switch to a national card."

B of A's Larkin commented, "First we had to do our thing [bank cards]. And then, after we had done it, we had to tell people what we had done. We had to educate, and with education came a greater tolerance and demand for the product itself. I think that what is happening is that banks are coming into their own as the purveyors of consumer credit. And other people are getting out and glad to get out; to leave the field to the bankers . . ."

The way that will happen is with "education"—concentrated, slick, expensive advertising and publicity campaigns pointing out all of the advantages of electronic banking. You will save money, the communications will promise. Life will be easier, they will pledge. Your money will be safer, they will assure. You will have more time to enjoy yourself (to spend more money), they will encourage.

To many people it will make sense. When that starts to happen, another campaign will appear. It will ask you why those bad old lawmakers won't let you have all of this new freedom, safety, time, and security. It will state the banks could do a better job for you at a lower price if all of those legal tie-downs weren't restricting them. It will add that you are a proud independent American, that you are smart about your money, and that you don't need some foggy heads in Foggy Bottom to tell you how to live your life. That will be backed up with some bank-developed figures showing that "99% of all borrowers and cardholders know how to handle their money responsibly."

In putting together this information, presented from their point of view, the banks will be enlisting you to support their antilegislation stand. They know that you, as a voter, are the key to preventing new laws which could bind them up even tighter and that with your help they might even be able to get some of the existing laws changed or thrown out. One of the major topics of the credit card bankers' 1980 "convention" was making the 1980's "the era of deregulation." Under specific banker attack are the EFT and individual state usury laws.

As Dee Hock said a couple of years ago, "We are not dismayed by preposterous laws and cumbersome regulations, for the law ever follows and never leads the marketplace. Even the government must yield to the will of the people and [with reverence] customers want bank-card service."

In some ways, it was the ultimate expression of democracy in action. You get to vote for a president only every four years.

You get to vote for the banks, the electronic money system, and the Lifebank Society every day, every time you use your bank card.

9

Cheating at Cards

ᴴE ᴡᴀꜱ ᴀʙᴏᴜᴛ as memorable as a coach-class airline meal. Medium-sized, medium coloring, hair and eyes "brownish," suit "grayish," face "like everyone's," as a few airline employees tried to recall. Yet, this brownish-grayish man will always be remembered at the Oakland, California, airport as the individual who set up his own highly successful ticket brokerage, purchasing expensive one-ways and round trips at full price, turning around and selling them at half price, and pocketing the proceeds. His secret of success? A series of fraudulent credit cards. Working five different counters of a leading international airline, he would wait for a flight to be called, line up, and purchase a ticket at the first counter, then move swiftly to the back of the line at the fifth counter. There, he would buttonhole a traveler waiting to purchase a similar ticket. Appealing to that person's greed for a bargain, he would peddle the ticket. If the lines were long, he could pull this resale fraud several times for one flight. In fact, he was so sure of himself that one time he not only sold a long-distance ticket to a willing buyer but took an order for an additional connecting flight and went off and got it.

Eventually he was caught. When news of his lone-wolf discount travel agency reached a group of fourteen people in New York, they shook their collective heads over the man's innocence. For nearly a year this group, using dozens of stolen credit cards and "squads" of runners, had purchased scores of transcontinental and international airline tickets and travel packages on custom order from individuals, teams, clubs, and organizations. New York to Rome, two weeks in St. Thomas including hotel, around the world—no order was too difficult to fill. When the scheme was finally uncovered, one confronted purchaser said, "Our club used them to go to Hawaii and back. The guy told us it was a special airline promotion fare."

Airlines were stuck with millions of dollars' worth of stolen or fraudulently charged tickets. Many stolen tickets are purchased with fraudulent cards or through fake travel agencies. Pan American World Airways once admitted it paid some $60,000 to a go-between (believed to be an organized-crime contact) to get back 2,000 blank airline tickets. It was a bargain. These tickets could have cost the airline a million dollars if used through the black market.

In Chicago, a seemingly pleasant and able waiter in one of that city's finest restaurants would pick up the patron's credit card and tab and disappear into the back room, ostensibly to run the card through the imprinter and then return with the voucher ready for signature. While at the imprinter, however, he would rapidly run another half-dozen blank vouchers through the machine, then later forge the diner's signature to them. These vouchers were then sold for varying amounts on the open underground markets, were used for everything from purchasing air conditioners to renting a car, which was then illegally sold.

In Houston, a motherly-looking woman wearing a smart tweed suit and sensible shoes used a stolen credit card and a counterfeit driver's license for identification to open a checking account. Once opened, with a minimum $300 deposit, she went out and wrote checks for over $18,000 against that account before the alarm went out and the funds dried up.

Ever since the early 1950's, when Diners Club promoted the idea of enjoying yourself now and paying later, a certain percentage of the population has been cleverly at work avoiding the *later*.

"It may not look like money, smell like money, or fold like money, but it spends like money," one credit-card crook reported, "so I spend it."

Another one said, "I used to use a little piece of plastic to shiv [open] doors and boost [burgle] a house. Now I use these plastics [cards] to boost department stores, airlines, everything."

So widespread has credit card fraud become that at one point BankAmericard and local law-enforcement personnel found a highly organized gang of over 400 credit card criminals operating in the Los Angeles area. Probing deeper, the investigators learned that if you knew where to go in that city you could get a complete "credit kit," consisting of counterfeit credit cards and other identification papers, plus a good credit rating in a national data bank. These credit ratings were slipped into files and computers by members of the ring who were employed as clerks in banks, department stores, and even in the data bank offices.

"Obviously," summed up one of the security officials, "it took us a long time to catch up with them. The data bank is considered the final judge of who is creditworthy, who pays their bills, and who is a fraud. If the computer reports somebody's okay, we usually don't check any further."

The fraud was not limited to individuals and small gangs, either. In Vincent Theresa's book, *My Life in the Mafia*, he admitted that "the mob stole Miami blind" with hot credit cards. They bought clothing, meals, rented cars, entertained, paid for their entire vacations with stolen cards. To top it off, they also made arrangements with store owners and others to bill fraudulent charges and split the bank-supplied income with them.

Throughout the country, there is a continuing cops-and-robbers battle to keep credit card fraud under control. On the one side, credit card companies and credit-data companies spend hundreds of thousands of dollars on personnel and communications and technical equipment to keep the systems tamperproof. On the other side, the credit card crooks keep finding cracks in the system and mining them for gold. Today, credit card fraud losses are at "an expected and manageable level," according to a Visa spokesman. Bank card officials admit a $95.5 million loss to fraud in 1979, expected that figure to be $138.9 million in 1980, and to run at about one-half of one percent of the total volume ($100 billion) in the near future. Master Charge reported similar figures and estimated that fraud losses would remain at between .37% and .65% in the future. However, newer figures show fraud losses could be running 1% or more. Insiders scoff at the official figures, say losses are already over $1 billion a year.

"Someone has to make up for it," says an executive of Visa, "and I'm afraid that someone is the cardholder—you—because of additional costs which we will have to pass on as charges. Fraud is, in total, a multibillion-dollar business, and someone has to pay for it."

During the infamous fraud-ridden period of the Chicago banks' entrance into the card business, those organizations were badly hit when thieves stole cards from the mail. So heavily did fraud cut into bank income that Continental's first-half earnings went down about $200,000 from the previous year, First National's dropped approximately $1.25 million, and Harris Trust's second-quarter profits dropped more than 9% "due to fraudulent use of cards." A U.S. postal official unofficially totaled all bank losses at $12 million.

One bank officer, totaling up the losses his organization had suffered issuing those credit cards, telephoned his advertising agency and asked that they scrap the existing campaign and replace it with another. "All in all," he said, "the way things have been going, we here at the bank don't quite agree with our slogan, 'The Nicest Thing Since Money.'"

Stealing cards from the mail and using them before the intended cardholder realized what was going on was one of the earliest and simplest forms of credit card fraud. Today, wily credit-card thieves use a mixed bag of tricks, including highly technologically advanced computer "tapping" to steal from the systems and from you.

Security forces working for credit card issuers say that there are some two dozen general categories in which credit card crooks work, and the list starts with the old Chicago-born thefts of credit cards by employees of the postal service. Despite the fact that banks now reissue credit cards on a year-round basis instead of mass "dropping" in one mailing, cards are still stolen somewhere in the sender-to-receiver system. Enterprising clerks, recognizing the card envelopes (despite the banks' attempts to disguise them as "plain-brown" types), can pick up impressive amounts of extra income by pocketing some of these mailings and selling them to always available "fences" on the street. Using the card within a short time period (usually forty-eight hours) and keeping purchases under $50, a professional credit card thief can run up bills of close to $10,000 without trying. Although computers are programmed to pick up signals and warn operators about unusual buying habits, these purchases never get to the computer because the card is not checked due to the low purchase figures.

Some users of the stolen cards have worked out a system to extend the "safe" forty-eight hours for days, weeks, or even months. Working with a confederate in the store or stores, the holder of the stolen card continues checking with that ally to see when the card number has been put on the "hot sheet" of stolen cards. When that number finally appears, that's when the card is dropped.

One unusually enterprising stolen-card user would wait for the constantly busy card's number to appear on the stolen-card list and then peddle it for $25 (below the then going street price of $50–$100) to a fellow thief. Not only was the additional money to the good, but in several cases the buyer was picked up by the police on his first attempt to use the card and charged with all of the purchasing fraud that had gone on before.

Another stolen-card user, informed that the card number had made the hot sheet, would merely drop the card in a public place, like a bus station, with the same hopes that an amateur would pick it up, use it, and be blamed for all the previous thefts.

One noted credit card con man, named "Mickey" Bryson, bilked credit card companies of up to $100,000 a year simply by having cards officially issued. Rummaging through trash containers behind stores, Bryson would pick up discarded credit card sales receipts or carbons. From these he would get the name, account number, and possibly the address of the cardholder. He would then go to the county census book to get background information on the individual. Armed with that information, he would then apply for a new credit card in that person's name, saying that the cardholder had moved to a new address. That address was a "drop" (usually a friend's apartment) where Bryson picked up his mail. After receiving a new card, he would arrange through other friends for a bogus driver's license. With the new card and that license he could use the credit for up to two months before the card went on an "unpaid, pick-up-card" list. In cases where he wanted to use the card longer, Bryson merely paid the first month's billing in full, thereby establishing a good credit rating on the card.

Bryson also obtained cards by "creating" people. Usually he chose a respectable professional title for the nonexistent person, knowing that common credit practice is not to delve too deeply into the finances of "doctors" or "lawyers" for fear of embarrassing them. For credit references, he would list Sears, Penney's, and furniture stores, because these companies will generally not divulge names or status of their credit cardholders. Using a false address, Bryson would gather dozens of these cards, have supplemental identification devices made up, and go on shopping sprees. An average year for Bryson was $50,000, and several years ran upward of $100,000 from purchased-then-resold goods and services. On top of that, he stayed in the finest hotels, ate at the best restaurants, traveled extensively, and lived a totally first-class life until he was caught.

Because of computer warning systems and widely distributed hot sheets and telephone clearance on some purchases, stolen credit cards do not have quite the value they used to enjoy. For years, burglars knew that credit cards were as good as cash, headed for the dresser drawers, where people usually keep their credit cards. Other burglars worked vacation and resort areas, waited for people to go to the swimming pool, then would raid their room and their wallet or purse for cash and credit cards. Prostitutes always knew they could earn an extra $25 to $200 on each credit card stolen from their customers and then peddled on the street. These ladies of the evening once accounted for 40% of all stolen cards. Pickpockets and purse snatchers also found a lucrative new market in credit cards.

Today, as "Mickey" Bryson discovered, the slickest, hardest-to-uncover, yet easiest way to get a fraudulent credit card is by creating a "person." Studies show that one out of every ten to twenty false applications is approved. Some security agents at Visa and MasterCard admit that the banks and the central clearing operations are notoriously sloppy about checking applications. More importantly, although the credit card companies loudly deny this, those same studies show that checking out every application can be more costly than living with the fraud losses originating with the professional credit card thieves.

A large percentage of credit card business is done by telephone or mail order. Using valid names and telephone numbers or addresses from carbon copies of sales tickets picked out of trash barrels, clever crooks can order thousands of dollars' worth of merchandise by telephone or mail, have it dropped at a rented or temporary address, then resell it. They take small chance of discovery, because the name and the number of the card are accurate, just as they are registered on the computer, and just as they have already been approved by the merchants. In one case, which chagrined security executives don't like to discuss, 879 shipments of different kinds of merchandise were sent to P.O. Box 787 at zip code 46799. That address turned out to be the state penitentiary in Lukesville, Ohio.

The system can work another way, too. Where there are thousands of recorded cases of mail-order shipments being sent to nonexistent or fraudulent purchasers, there are also cases of mail-order merchants reversing the scam, robbing the credit card companies through the cardholders. Visa, MasterCard, Diners and Carte Blanche were victimized for about $500,000 by a Thomas A. Constantine who ran a mail-order jewelry business called Constantine Gems. Constantine advertised exceptionally low prices on jewelry by mail in national publications. The ads emphasized that the company accepted major credit cards. When orders came in, Constantine was careful to get immediate payment from the card companies, but the jewelry he sent out, when he sent it out, was not nearly the quality described in the ads. Faced with complaints and impending legal action, Constantine went into court and declared bankruptcy, leaving the credit card companies stuck with the half-million dollars in disputed cardholder claims and refunds.

In another case, a Philadelphia-based company built up a large file of creditworthy card customers by offering an executive résumé service for $35. Eventually the organization used that file of names to create false sales slips and by adding another "0" to the amount, made each charge $350. Using the same scheme on dozens of banks in Atlanta, Philadelphia, Chicago, San Antonio, and dozens of other locations, the résumé service ran up fraudulent charges of over $3 million, which the banks must make good.

More demanding than stolen cards, fraudulent applications, and mail and telephone deceptions, is the counterfeit- or altered-credit-card scam, yet it is one of the more popular ways to steal from the credit card systems. Even though the "moneyless society" appears to be more and more a reality, improved security measures on card counterfeiting or alteration haven't come along. The engraving of currency and the printing of checks is filled with tight security measures to protect those forms of money. However, virtually any printer who can get access to polyvinyl plastic blanks or sheets and an embossing machine can set himself up as a credit card producer.

At a plant in Maspeth, New York, that embosses credit cards, two employees went into business for themselves and embossed 1,500 duplicate cards, which they sold to organized-crime representatives. Resulting loss to the credit card company was $621,000.

In Massachusetts, an employee whose job was storing stocks of plastic cards wrote to Master Charge executives saying that he had 60,000 blank cards he would sell to them for $37,500. He and an accomplice were tracked down and arrested, to the enormous relief of Master Charge officials. They estimated that those 60,000 cards, if processed and circulated, could have caused losses up to $15 million. One professional says that figure is low, that in the hands of slick professional card passers, it could easily have reached $30 million.

The employee knew that blank credit cards have no number, no name, no identifying device, and that security precautions go into place only later, after the cards have been imprinted. Because of this, the tracing of missing credit card blanks is almost impossible. Even if inventory shows that a box or two are gone, it could be a mix-up in shipment, a misplaced bulk container, or even a mistake on the bill of lading. For that reason, there is seldom an investigation of missing card blanks, despite the fact that blanks are extremely valuable to large, organized groups that have their own stamping equipment and nationwide fraudulent-card-distribution systems.

Counterfeit cards are dangerous not only because of their credit purchasing power but also because, in today's increasingly complex electronic money society, cards can be used to withdraw cash, transfer money between accounts, and even borrow money.

It is for those potentially much more rewarding reasons that credit criminals stay busy developing new ingenious ways to counterfeit or alter cards which will work for merchandise in stores, for cash in automated cash machines, and for bank accounts from which cash can be withdrawn.

Successful counterfeiting of cards would require a great deal of inside information and knowledge. Usually it would require one or more people who can get the names and account numbers of creditworthy cardholders, generally from the files or computers of a credit card issuing bank. Next, the ideal counterfeiting ring would have someone who knew the technical requirements of manufacturing credit cards and an artist who specialized in silk-screen printing. Finally, an outside salesperson or group would be needed for selling, distributing, using, and syndicating the completed credit cards. Equipment necessary would include the plastic blanks, silk-screen reproduction process, and imprinting or embossing machines.

The credit card counterfeiters who have all of this personnel and/or equipment are turning out such a good product these days that they are sometimes detected because they are *better* than the authentic cards.

For years, counterfeits suffered from bad silk-screen printing, which made them easy to spot. In 1978, a new nine-step silk-screen process was described in an underground newspaper and explained so simply that even high school students could easily get into the fake card business. That same newspaper even relayed complete details on adding the fake signature panel and "protective" magnetic stripe common to most credit cards.

At about the same time the article appeared, excellent counterfeits were turning up in California, Texas, Florida, and other high-credit-usage states. Most of the counterfeiters had started with the Visa card because of its simple blue-white-gold bars design. Experts say that the next simplest to duplicate are Carte Blanche and Diners cards. MasterCard, with its overlapping different-colored circles, is considered more difficult to copy, and the American Express card, with its busy background, is considered the toughest. Readership of the underground newspaper that described the new silk-screen process must have been extensive. Investigators even found evidence that some fake Master Charge (its name at the time) cards were coming out of a thriving cottage industry located in a Georgia prison.

Altering cards has become another device used to bilk the banks and the credit card industry. In one case, more than a million dollars was made on cards obtained from bartenders, prostitutes, and petty thieves. The cards were changed with a "shave-and-paste" method. Within minutes, an expert "shaver" can smooth off or change the raised letters on a card and imprint or paste on new ones. These particular cards were used to buy airline tickets, which were then resold for half price. This system was almost impossible to detect until the phony charges were made and billed. It was only then that the confused mixture of cardholder names with incorrect numbers showed up and detective work was initiated.

Testifying before a committee investigating credit-card fraud, a criminal called Todd explained his personal way of altering cards.

"I gently heated all the cards I had collected, using the catalyst from polyester resin to remove the ink identifying the old owners, pressed the cards with a warm iron to flatten them, shaved off with a razor blade any remaining unevenness, and on Saturday afternoons made the rounds of the printing departments of Sears, J. C. Penney's, Macy's, Kaiser, and the University of California Medical Center, using their addressographs, stamping new names and numbers into my cards, ignoring the blanks that were available to me at each place in favor of the heavier cards I had brought with me."

Todd also claimed that at other times, in need of cards, he simply walked into the mailing department of several credit card-issuing companies. Dressed casually, in shirt sleeves, he pretended to be an employee, nonchalantly picked up bunches of stamped envelopes containing credit cards from unattended desks, and walked out.

Todd also walked away with up to $5,000 cash a day, using altered cards to exploit weaknesses in the credit card system. Carrying an attaché case and dressed as a conservative businessman, Todd would make his rounds of banks. At some he would apply for a "cash advance" on a fake credit card and receive it. At others he would use stolen blank checks to make a sizable withdrawal, and verify the fake signature on the check with the same fake signature on an altered credit card. Todd would invest additional time plundering the retail shops in tourist sections, where clerks rarely bother to check cards closely because sales are usually under $50 and because they handle so many out-of-town cards. Touring rapidly from store to store, Todd would load up on clothing, radios, camera equipment, and other easily sold merchandise. When he had enough, Todd would sell the newly purchased items at a lower price to tourists and pedestrians on the streets, and what he had left over at day's end he would dump to a professional fence who dealt in stolen goods.

Todd admitted he didn't have much respect for so-called security systems. When caught with a fake, misused, or altered card, Todd would bully suspicious clerks with loud threats of false arrest. They would usually return the card, let him go. One time, however, a clerk, who refused to be intimidated, called the store's security guards. Todd left the scene quickly but hid behind another counter, keeping an eye on his wristwatch. It took 12 minutes and 38 seconds before the house cops arrived, which, as someone noted, "was enough time to leisurely rob the place with a gun. With that time span, who needs to alter credit cards?"

These credit card thieves found weaknesses in the credit card system through either a change in the *person* who uses the card or a change in the *card* itself. However, a new breed of highly sophisticated criminal is now attacking the heart of the credit card business—the electronic system which makes it possible. This system has terminals, communications networks, computers, and computer programs. Each step of the system is under constant probing by credit criminals looking for weaknesses that can mean instant wealth.

There are three types of terminals. The first, or "beginning of the line," is known as a *manned terminal*, and it's the device you see bank employees use to punch up information. It's considered fairly secure because it's inside the bank, but its in-built weakness is the communications line that connects it with the bank's computer. If the bank computer, as often happens, makes a mistake on your account, it will show up on that terminal. That is usually an honest mistake, but it is this communications weakness which allows terminals to be manipulated by canny thieves. Since the terminal shows only what it is told by the computer, what would happen if another computer got into the communications line between the master computer and the terminal? It could easily show the teller that you had $35,000 in your account instead of $35—because the intruding computer was programmed to pass on that false information. The terminal doesn't know, it only shows what it gets.

Generally, any terminal can be "tapped" by cutting a mini-computer into the telephonelike lines. The terminal known as an *automated teller* can be ordered to dump all of its available cash into the withdrawal drawer by a clever thief with a basic knowledge of computer systems. In some cases, banks have attempted to head this off by having the main computer "watch" the terminal for any unusual activity. The thief thwarts that by having his mini-computer signal the bank computer that everything's okay, while at the same time it is signaling the automated teller to fork over everything it's got.

A fast-moving, smart teller-tapper can pocket as much as 4,000 new bills (usually tens and twenties) from each machine, and the chances of being caught are fairly small. Frighteningly enough, some new machines will carry cartridges containing 12,000 new bills; $120,000 in tens or $240,000 in twenties.

The third terminal is a *point-of-sale* device on which store clerks punch up sales and get an okay on the credit card. Here, the mini-computer can be put into the communications line to cut off reject signals on lost or stolen cards, and, instead, to give the sales clerk a clearance.

Communications lines to terminals can also be tapped to raid the main computer of lists of creditworthy names and card numbers and other information which can help the criminal drain the system.

Computer systems can also be programmed for grander schemes.

Using "certain sounds, signals, and writings," three people were charged with fraudulently transferring $433,000 from First National Bank of New Jersey to the Carteret branch of the Perth Amboy National Bank of New Jersey. The clever threesome was also charged with opening a checking account in fictitious names and transferring $2 million from the First National City Bank of New York to First National Bank of New Jersey and into a "company" account. All of this was done through computer tapping.

Although the main computer is usually heavily guarded and highly secure, this heart of the credit card system is still vulnerable to certain highly sophisticated forms of tapping. Information can be inserted or withdrawn; fake names can be made "real" people; valuable lists of real people can be stolen, and funds can be manipulated. The computer's greatest weakness is its vulnerability to the humans who work with it. Dishonest employees can insert or extract material, giving criminal associates a computerized-theft process. Since the computer is considered the final authority on good versus bad cards, the creditworthy versus the criminal, what it says goes. If it carries falsely implanted information, those data become "truth" all along the communications line. It's a fact that modern high-speed computers are capable of *stealing one million times a second*. The potential for enormous financial rewards—to the brilliant criminal—is staggering. The purchasing power of credit cards of all kinds in the United States could reach $500 billion by 1985. Buying power on Visa and MasterCard alone was running close to $64 billion a year in early 1980 and is headed for an estimated $175 billion by 1985. Any or all of that immense financial depository (in the form of electronic exchange) can be tapped, is being tapped, and will continue to be tapped by criminal minds thinking ahead and moving faster than the ordinary cumbersome security methods employed by the banks and the credit-card systems.

As an illustration of how even the best systems have weaknesses, the American Bankers Association gave its blessing to a protective device called the mag (for magnetic) stripe in 1971. The mag stripe, according to its fans, was the definitive answer to credit card fraud. It contained specially encoded information on a dark stripe usually located on the back of a credit card. That information was "read" by a terminal which transmitted the data to a central computer which either okayed the card or sent out a warning signal. According to plan, the mag stripe would (a) get rid of the "floor limit" of $50 which demands that clerks call in for an okay for purchases over that amount, (b) head off altered cards by reporting the original, unaltered card number to the computer, and (c) spot stolen or lost cards immediately because of the speed of electronics, as compared to manually made-up and distributed hot sheets and warning lists.

Although the rest of the banking industry was generally enthusiastic about the mag stripe, Citibank didn't share the confidence in the stripe. John R. Scantlin, chairman of Transaction Technology, Inc., a Citibank subsidiary, decided to test it. He invited twenty-two teams of students from the California Institute of Technology to override the mag stripe, to discover its weaknesses. Prize money was $15,000, and he ended up paying out twenty-two prizes.

Did it require extraordinarily complex electronic devices to do this? Not at all. One expert commented, "A sophomore-level electrical-engineering student could build himself at least four or five different devices for reading the mag stripe on a card out of a handful of scraps lying around the electrical-engineering lab." When asked if that sophomore would first have to know exactly how the card had been encoded, he replied, ". . . this information is floating around all the college campuses in the United States—just as they circulated plans for that 'little blue box' to wipe out the phone system. . ." That infamous gadget had been developed by enterprising students to make untraceable (and therefore unbillable) phone calls to any place in the world.

Since then, the mag stripe has been made more secure but is still not in universal use. Smaller banks do not have the technology or the vast investment needed to install the entire magnetic stripe system. Too, other banks feel that the mag stripe is not the answer, and before investing heavily in it, are awaiting a better, more foolproof system.

Citibank developed its own system for cards. Each card contained a "magic middle" made up of fifty-five rectangles in a grid. These rectangles were encoded with information, and when the card was put into a terminal, an infrared beam "read" the rectangles and converted them to electronic impulses. The major advantage of these Citibank cards was that they could be produced cheaply but attempts to reproduce them were very costly. The major disadvantage was that the Citibank card needed a special terminal to read it, and most retail stores and other locations with terminals were equipped with standard ones.

Tomorrow looks no better. One of the foundations of the coming electronic funds transfer system is shared banking terminals in a national network. Organized crime could easily tap these systems to get credit files, personal identification codes, and other information which would make it simple to loot and ravage the bank card system. Federal law-enforcement investigators have found that some financial institutions are owned or controlled by organized crime, and these firms could provide automatic access to the supposedly secure secrets of the other financial institutions.

No one knows how extensive computer crime is. The FBI was reported as saying that only one percent of all computer crimes are detected, only fourteen percent of these are ever reported, and only three percent of cases result in jail terms!

In addition to the professional and amateur criminals, there are other individuals and groups motivated to steal from the banks for political or ideological reasons. A while ago, one underground magazine carried these words:

> It is also important from a revolutionary perspective to make sure you are keeping from and burning the enemy [banks], not the people. So try fancy places, getting into high class places, we want you to hit the man [banks], not the people. . . . On the shopping end make sure you are hitting big chain stores and exclusive places aside from the correctness of it, you may as well get the best if you are shopping this way . . . If you are really serious about destroying the man [banks], why should you contribute to his survival by paying for anything. When you get a credit card, use it a lot. Buy stuff for friends, buy stuff you don't need, and sock it to him. Phony credit cards and check purchases destroy the concept of credit, without which capitalism cannot survive, so hit the man where it hurts him, in his pocket book.

One of the reasons credit card fraud continues as a major crime is that, historically, credit card companies, banks, retailers, oil companies, airlines, etc., have refused to join in a concerted effort to wipe out that fraud. They refused to cooperate with organizations like the International Association of Credit Card Investigators, which offered to set up a central clearinghouse for fraud information. Rivalry between Visa and MasterCard, between American Express and Diners and Carte Blanche, rivalry between department stores with their own credit cards and the bank cards, all stand in the way of one concentrated effort.

Philip H. Wynn, deputy district attorney in the Major Fraud Division, Los Angeles district attorney's office, once said, "Since September, 1975, I have been actively involved in the prosecution of computer crime. . . I have discovered no system is failsafe and this is especially disturbing considering our increasing dependence upon computers for day-to-day existence. My exposure to the computer community has convinced me security is one of the last factors they consider. So long as profit and loss statements are positive, management does not want to face the prospect of a major security breach or spend the money to deter it."

That may well be. Computer tapping could easily become the equivalent of robbing a hundred Fort Knoxes in the very near future. So long as the bankers and the credit card officials remain fairly complacent about the situation, highly educated and clever credit card criminals will continue to find cracks in the system, faults in the financial setups, which can be highly rewarding to them. Right now, even as this country's smartest engineers work on newer and better methods to protect the electronic money system and the credit card industry, other brilliant people, with less of an altruistic bent, are working to beat those systems before they are even in place.

Brightest hope for some form of unbeatable system is a card which actually contains a type of semi-conductor memory chip right within the card. The advantage of this card is that it can store much more data than a magnetic stripe, and the more data a card contains, the more secure it can be made. Advanced development work on this form of card started in Europe, and some bankers and, of course, electronics companies are plumping for it here. One discouraged security man, however, feels that even the chip card will have its security chipped away by ultraingenious thieves.

And on the lower, nonelectronic level, cleverness continues too. Recently, a woman named Patricia Eigenrauch was killed by a Chicago commuter train. Although her husband canceled her cards immediately, he received credit-card invoices for $765 from Saks and Lord & Taylor department stores. All purchases were made after her death.

Card fraud. It's a multibillion-dollar business, and as the man said, "Someone has to pay for it."

The banks don't.

Guess who does.

10

The Right to No

THE CREDIT PEOPLE of the bank-card business don't quite know how to break their bad news, so here it is. What they want you to know is that you have no real right to privacy. Informational privacy. Facts about your income, your booze tolerance, your age, illnesses, school grades, military derring-do, arrests and convictions, voting record, and how you spend your money are not, repeat, are not protected by any court-approved, police-enforced constitutional sentence, paragraph, section, or amendment. If you think privacy is something you have coming to you, what you actually have coming to you is a disappointment, according to them.

Professor Christopher H. Pyle of the City University of New York commented, "In many respects, [privacy] is little more than a deeply felt sentiment that individuals ought to have more control over what others are told about them than they do now. Constitutionally, the right to privacy tends to be a derivative right—a right which exists to serve other rights and interests and which is, on many occasions, subordinated to other interests."

The law being as vague as it is, some legislators claim that Articles One, Three, Four, Five, Nine, Ten, and Fourteen of the amendments to the Constitution "protect the constitutional rights of privacy of individuals concerning whom identifiable information is recorded." The bankers say there is grave doubt about their stance. These amendments do set up certain protections from forms of intrusion from other people and from the government, the bankers admit, but there is no *definitive* statement about your right to privacy from snoopers. If that right is in those glorious pages somewhere, it is so loosely and ambiguously worded it's close to impossible to dig out.

If they are right, it is undoubtedly an idea which crossed no one's mind in the days of the Continental Congress. Back then, in those small settlements, everyone's business was everybody's, and local gossip hardly seemed like constitutional fodder. Townspeople knew who were the Tories, who drank too much ale, who was seen hanging around Paul's wife while he was off selling Revere Ware. Those topics hardly belonged with such lofties as forming a more perfect union, establishing justice, providing for the common defense . . .

Today, in our bloated societies, that type of personal information is limited to families, co-workers, neighborhoods, and our modern-day town gossip, the computer. Without shading or coloring the stories, without ever being scandalized, the computer just repeats what it hears—magnetic in and magnetic out over the electronic back fences of the world.

But even if your forefathers had guaranteed privacy, many bankers feel that they have a stronger right and that is the *right to know* (often called the right to no by those whose credit applications have been rejected). They say that existing ideas of privacy are just custom and habit and have no basis in fact and in law, whereas information is a "right" in a free country. Summed up, their attitude toward information about you is that everything that is not prohibited is authorized. After all, they say, isn't that what government does?

Yes. You do not have to be a Communist, a veteran, a tax-evader, or a suspected presidential assassin to be magnetically encoded in the hundreds of federal data banks. If you've ever put money in a bank, made an insurance claim, paid a tax, received welfare or unemployment insurance, paid Social Security, gone to school, been written up in the newspaper, or just held a salaried job, you're in there, and privacy is something you're going to have to get in the bathroom.

For example, the bank secrecy act requires that those institutions make available to the government many financial transactions of their customers, including any checking ones over

$100, and the Medicaid Management Information System pays the states a bonus if they turn over highly detailed patient files for inspection by federal investigators. And even top-level officials aren't safe. "I read all five of his FBI files, and there's not a bad line in any of them. I've never read such files, he's just a straight arrow," U.S. Attorney General Griffin Bell said one day. Was he talking about you, me? No, he was referring to the information recorded on a man whose records should have been totally secure, FBI Director William H. Webster.

Senator Sam Ervin of North Carolina once commented, "When I came to the Senate in 1954, computers were practically unheard of and information about individuals was stored, if at all, in filing cabinets. . . . Now information about each individual American is contained in literally hundreds of computerized files, both governmental and private. . ."

For years the Internal Revenue Service has supplied supposedly confidential computer tapes of tax information to individual states so they might catch up with local evaders. Daily the FBI computers chatter incessantly with police departments throughout the nation. The Justice Department, Secret Service, Army Counterintelligence, dozens of other governmental bureaus maintain extensive dossiers on activists, troublemakers, and protesters, all programmed or computerized. Throughout the government, most of our other citizenry has been captured and trussed up in brown magnetic tape or held captive in file drawers.

Awed by such efficiency and thoroughness in privacy invasion, the bankers took the government's example both to heart and to their computer rooms. After all, hadn't the Supreme Court itself struck down a pathway of legal protection for privacy? In the case of U.S. vs. Miller, which was decided in 1976, that august body decided that the individual person had no "legitimate expectation of privacy" against the government with respect to personal records held by another party.

Originally, local banks had small computers which checked out local bank-card customers. Later, when regional bank card setups came about, larger computers and more intricate networks were developed. Today, both Visa and MasterCard's massive international networks can connect your card-clearance center with just about any signed-up merchant in the world, with credit bureaus, with other financial institutions. Because the two bank cards have been made into international buying devices or a form of worldwide value exchange, the bankers want to make sure, very sure, that their computer files are accurate and that you're good for the money.

How does a bank card official go about deciding whether to lend you their money in the form of a bank card, and if so, how much? With information about you. The traditional three C's of credit are Capital (how much you have), Capacity (how much you earn or could make), and Character (do you or would you pay your bills). The more information, the better. This information is around, has been all of your life. In past years, it was located in many places: hospitals, personnel offices, schools, the military, tax files, city halls. Now most of that information has been stacked, indexed, collated, and assembled into a personal profile, and the banker is looking to see whether you're a mug shot or a matinee idol.

Originally, many professional fact-finders, the snoopers, left no stone that they could throw at you unturned. They interviewed neighbors, got cozy with bartenders, dated your ex, bought drinks for your boss, in order to get the real lowdown from the lowdown's point of view. All of that information became part of the record. Today, with new restricting legislation, they are limited, theoretically, to finding out what kind of a credit risk you are. Some do, some don't.

Private credit information about you is warehoused in companies called credit-reporting services or bureaus. There are over two thousand of these file holders in the country, some local, some national. Together, they have over 200 million files. One of the giants, TRW Credit Data, admits it has files on over 70 million people, but one authority says the figure is closer to 110 million. These reports show when and where you opened accounts, how you paid, when you ran into financial trouble, how you handled it, whether you're employed, and other information a bank card executive would need to judge whether you're plastic-worthy. At TRW, other information can include Social Security number, income, age, and other bits of your life you may have put down on a credit application at some time. What is not supposed to be included in your credit file are sex, religion, marital status, and criminal record.

However, TRW files, like other credit-information storehouses, are made up of data supplied by its customers—by the banks and businesses that use it. If one of those supposedly forbidden items should just happen to be part of an incoming record, chances are good it will be transferred and become part of TRW's file as well.

So complete are the files at TRW, and some other credit bureaus, that the FBI and other government agencies actually purchase data on individuals from those companies. To protect itself and to comply with legislation, TRW and the others say they demand a court order before they can release those files. One official admits, though, that it wasn't too long ago that a government agent could flash a badge or make a phone call and be up to his shoulder holster in information about you or anyone else.

These credit bureaus do not decide whether you get credit or not, make no determination about your risk rating. They do categorize the files into "positive," "negative," or "nonevaluative," but it is up to the bank card people to make the final decision. The tentacles of outfits like TRW reach a long way. You may leave behind mate and kiddies and move to some hamlet God forgot, but TRW won't. They'll find you faster than dandruff finds blue serge. That's one of the prime places law-enforcement agencies can pick up cold trails; that's the one location where the Bent Fork general store can find out you still owe money in Chicago.

For years, getting credit was a matter of personal judgment. Some credit manager decided whether he liked the cut of your jib or your job, and that was it. Not anymore. Because of the physical impossibility of personally interviewing every single prospect for a bank card, plus tight legislation which prevents turndowns because of sex or age or other items, a great percentage of the credit givers have gone to a system called "scoring."

Scoring systems are based on a variable group of standards which may or may not include your age, marital status, number of dependents, whether you rent or own, how long you've held your job and have lived at an address, take-home pay, monthly bills, occupation, and other facts. Each item has a numerical value. By adding up, man or machine can decide whether to pass you on or to pass on you.

Computers are programmed to sift these values and assign points or numbers to them. For example, if 1,000 bad applications, 1,000 credit rejections, and 1,000 good applications are introduced into the computer, it can electronically analyze the differences, sort out the good prospects from the fakes and the deadbeats. Generally, the computer is not given the total go/no-go authority. There is a marginal group of applications which require personal judgment. On a point-scoring system, obviously those rated between 70 or 80 and 100 would be granted a card. Those beneath 35, undoubtedly not. It is the group that falls into that large middle section that demands a decision by the bank card executive. The banks, of course, can move those parameters around whenever financial conditions change. In good profitable times when money is plentiful and cheap and losses are low, that turndown score of 35 might be reduced to 30 and the banks will chance the risk. In bad times, that lowest possible score might be raised to 50 or even higher.

At one time, credit was as easy as getting a card in the mail. Today, with high interest rates and potentially high losses, money is expensive and hard to get. According to the Los Angeles *Times*, since the bank card became a big-time spender, outstanding consumer debt has tripled, has grown one and one-third times faster than personal income. In the fall of 1979, you and other Americans owed a frightening total of $304 billion in installment debt, compared to just over $98 billion ten years before that. Of that, some $55 billion was owed on revolving credit cards of all types, and that was more than sixteen times what was owed just on revolving credit ten years earlier.

Today, with that kind of money being lent out, with money costing more, scoring systems are getting increasingly tougher.

There are other problems to credit scoring. Things change. A factory may cut back and leave its employees without income, thereby changing their credit scores. Another section of the bank might want to introduce a new kind of service demanding a different level of customer. Formulas for accepting good risks are constantly monitored. What is good for Bank of America one day could be sudden death for it tomorrow.

One of the most controversial areas in selecting the credit-worthy is "redlining," or the arbitrary refusal to accept anyone from a certain geographical section. Some insurance companies have been doing this for years with automobile coverage, but a few Washington folks don't like it. Senator Proxmire, who probed some important consumer interests and who has been behind much anti-card practice legislation, has attacked the practice. Other serious questions about scoring systems have been brewing with consumer advocates and the Federal Trade Commission. Most outspoken was Congressman Annunzio of the House Subcommittee on Consumer Affairs. Annunzio, whose traditional examinations of the credit card industry drove strong bankers to strong spirits, was most upset that no federal agency checked out the scoring practices of the credit industry. He believed that scoring is the "perfect system for discrimination without being caught," because no one outside knows what's going on. It's like students grading their own papers.

When an applicant is turned down for credit through the scoring system, that should be the end of it. It isn't. Traditionally, those rejected applications have become official record and part of the computer banks of the credit bureaus. One outfit called Credit Index compiled a file of over 16 million people who couldn't get credit, 16 million people who were rejected by most major credit givers. That's 16 million today. Tomorrow when the bank card is not an optional way to buy but just about the only way to survive, these people will not be able to get into Lifebank. They will survive only if the government sets up special programs for them.

These are the dis-credited. The computers say so. Certainly some belong there—the ripoff artists, the con men, the never-pay-it-back people. But there are others who are in those files because of suspicious scoring systems, because of faulty bank judgments, because of redlining, because of age or sex, or because some bankers don't feel they're profitable enough, people like newlyweds or the elderly who live on a small fixed income. Too, many of them might be in that financial Devil's Island purely because the computer made a mistake.

If a computer makes a mistake on a checking account, the bank knows the customer will complain. If a computer makes a mistake on a credit application, the person who wants the credit is turned away, generally doesn't know what to do. There was a time when what they could do was nothing. The time of tight "right to no" by the credit bureaus, by the banks. If you were turned down, you were SOL, as the Marines say.

But the legislators began hearing about it with bitter notes from home and letters that started out, "Dear Congressman, If you want a lot of credit, find out why I can't get mine . . ."

In the early 1970's, Health, Education and Welfare Secretary Elliott Richardson put together a committee which compiled a report called "Records, Computers, and the Rights of Citizens." In 1974, a Privacy Act was whipped through the lawmakers by Senator Sam Ervin. It put some controls on how information about people was collected and handled by departments and agencies of the government. One of the demands it made was for creation of a Privacy Protection Study Commission to look at the situation out in the private world and report back to the president and the Congress whether any of the rules in that bill should apply outside. In 1978, that report was issued. Its 650 pages came to some forceful conclusions about abuses of privacy in outside information-gathering and -handling. It made many suggestions for new laws to control these. The areas most clearly singled out for additional laws were credit reporting and credit giving.

Then, in 1976, another piece of legislation, the Freedom of Information Act, was passed. It gave you and others the right to dig into any and all government files to see what they had on you and what the government had been up to all these years.

Both acts were good-intentioned and had good results, but out of them came a questionable effect. The Privacy Act, which was limited to government agencies, restricted what the government could do with its files on you and others. Each bureau or department which had a file on you could not swap it with other government agencies unless you said it was okay. And the Freedom of Information Act said you could see your own files on demand. That meant you could ask to see everything the government had dredged up on you, and those files would all be brought together from various departments for your review. That way, with the computers sorting and sifting and collecting every bit of information, you could get the whole picture—but so could others. Before, with your files spread out, it was difficult for that to happen. The Freedom Act made it easy. A simple matter of cross-checking, by using just a few letters of your name or your driver's-license number, could reveal your entire federally assembled history. For the professional snoopers who know their way in and around information-gathering, it made things much easier.

Much of what computers turn out can be easily read or translated, even if it is pure data. For example, here are the hypothetical purchases made by two different bank-card holders for one month.

RICHARD M.
3 cases Dom Perignon champagne
1 repair bill, Brentwood Jaguar Service
3 nights' lodging and meals, Plaza Hotel, New York
1 Rolex watch
1 Pierre Cardin blazer

BILLY R.
10 six-packs beer
1 tune-up kit, Bob's Auto Supply
3 nights' lodging and meals, the Mint, Las Vegas
1 Timex watch
1 baseball jacket

If those two data sheets rattled out of the computer and onto a terminal in front of you, what could you tell about the two men? Which one would you want your daughter to marry?

There was other legislation which partially protected privacy. The Equal Credit Opportunity Act said among other things that creditors couldn't ask whether you intended to have children or were using birth-control methods.

Another law, the Fair Credit Reporting Act, demanded more privacy. It also gave you more information about yourself. With it, you could find out:

1. The information in your credit file and where it came from.

2. Who had received a copy of the file for credit use in the past six months or employment use in the past two years.

The Fair Credit Reporting Act further provided:

3. That the file was confidential and was to be given out only when you applied for a job or credit.

4. That any information you didn't agree with would be reinvestigated.

5. That any information which was wrong would be removed and anyone who had received the wrong information would be supplied with the right material.

6. That you could make up to a one-hundred-word statement giving your side of the story when there was a dispute and the investigation didn't solve it.

7. And, finally, that all bad information would be taken off the record if it was more than seven years old (or fourteen years in case of a bankruptcy).

Porous privacy was beginning to fill in. But all was not singing and dancing everywhere. With each move to protect your privacy, someone else felt mortally wounded.

Businesses set up a holler about the Freedom of Information Act because the trade secrets and confidential information which the government demanded were getting to their competitors. Too, criminals merely had to go to the files to find out who squealed on them.

Benjamin R. Civiletti, then deputy attorney general, took a stand, speaking for the Justice Department against new legislation set up to make sure your bank records are private. As projected, any law-enforcement agency would have to tell you it was going to look at your bank records, and if you objected within two weeks, they couldn't do it. Civiletti said that law would make it much too easy to obstruct justice.

The world-minded bankers are complaining today that the privacy laws which affect computers could also affect free enterprise between nations, because privacy laws vary in different parts of the world.

What could be ordinary information on you in Turkey could be privacy invasion at home, but the unediting computer would merely pass it along. Stabilizing information of this type between countries would be like stabilizing currencies. Instead, the American Bankers Association, trade association of the bankers, told the government that it should just set down general guidelines for privacy and let the bankers, in their wisdom, handle it from there.

"More self-regulation and voluntary implementation of general legislative objectives would be beneficial to all concerned, since it would begin to alleviate the inflationary effect of excessive regulations," that group said in a letter.

The bankers group has been very concerned about a new White House-supported bill, based on the recommendations of the Privacy Protection Study Commission. That bill has sections which add to privacy in an age of computers. It offers more protection on the collection, use, and distribution of information about people; ensures accuracy of the records and privacy in mail and other communications. It also examines how much the federal government should be interfering with private information systems.

Guaranteed accuracy and computer privacy are the big musts. In the past, computer accuracy and privacy have been a laugh. There are hundreds of examples. Here are a few:

A federal jury gave an Arkansas divorcée $255,000 in damages from the information bureau Equifax Inc. That firm had prepared an insurance report on her saying, incorrectly, that she had been living with a man for four months "without benefit of matrimony." She won the case based on her claim that the report violated the Fair Credit Reporting Act, which demands that companies like Equifax "assure maximum possible accuracy."

The same company, Equifax, which kept files on over 45 million people, was under investigation for three years. A Federal Trade Commission judge decided that the company had used "unfair and deceptive" practices in collecting information about customers, had failed to follow reasonable procedures to assure maximum possible accuracy of its records, had not erased or changed incorrect information, and had given reports out to unauthorized people. It turned out that some field investigators for Equifax were not only using unqualified sources of information but also even faking reports on people.

The District Court of Denver named a group of insurance companies for trying to use personal records in order to settle claims. The insurance firms hired a company called Factual Service Bureau of Denver to get secret credit card telephone code numbers so they could raid the computer files to get confidential medical information.

David Linowes, who was chairman of the U.S. Privacy

Protection Study Commission until late 1977, said that credit card companies were lax in protecting confidentiality of customer files and information was too often given out to investigators without challenging the request. He added that 90% of the time the government had obtained information from credit card companies by simply making a phone call. No record of the call or the transfer of data was kept at either end.

With all of these experts debating where personal privacy starts and stops, how do the people in the files feel? Depends on what you read.

In a 1979 privacy study conducted by the national opinion research firm of Louis Harris and Associates for Sentry Insurance Company, some 64% of people interviewed were concerned about threats to personal privacy and believed that we were close to George Orwell's "big brotherism" of 1984. They also believed that finance companies, credit bureaus, insurance companies, credit card companies, and the media were the biggest private invaders of privacy, in that order.

Reporting optimistically on the same study, *The American Banker* said, "Two-thirds of Americans believe that banks limit the personal information they gather on individuals to what is really necessary. . ." That was the opening of their story, and it was headlined "PUBLIC FINDS BANKS ARE NOT TOO CURIOUS." They carefully omitted the dual impact of banks and credit bureaus, in combination.

Actually, combining banks, credit card companies, *and* credit bureaus—all overlappingly involved in gathering or handling the same type of information for credit cards—the bank card business comes out of that study as the biggest single privacy threat.

Were the majority of bankers concerned? The same study showed that only 30% of those moneymen were. Poll conductor Harris commented, ". . . these leadership groups might profitably listen to the voices of the public as reflected in this survey, and they might then change their minds."

We are walled in with a network of connected computers, governmental and private. These linked information sources are growing technologically larger, more efficient, more all-knowing every day. These systems in themselves are not bad. A telephone line is not a liar, it is a telephone line. A computer is not a malicious reference, it is an electronic marvel. These information and communication systems are absolutely essential to keep our governments, our industries, our businesses, our societies operating. If we depended upon paper, the backed-up information would probably reach from here to 1945.

What these systems do not have is judgment and wisdom. In the days when we had only paperwork, humans prepared the information, humans reviewed it, humans made decisions. Today, although humans program the computers, it is much too easy for critical errors about us to become a matter of permanent record. Faked reports, prejudiced information, incorrect facts, are all magnetic-in/magnetic-out to the computer, and it reports all, humanizes nothing. Even though most of us know that we can review our credit record if we feel it contains bad information, a recent poll showed that over half of the people who felt wronged chose to do nothing about it. And with nothing being done, the computers continued to spit out incorrect information, dis-crediting those people from their proper place in the economy.

The Privacy Protection Study came up with a lot of finger-waggling and pointing-with-alarm. The study is on the side of Right and Truth and Honesty and Good. It said we should have a privacy-protection policy which minimizes intrusiveness "to create a proper balance between what an individual is expected to divulge to a record-keeping organization and what he seeks in return." It also recommended fairness "to open record-keeping operations" so individuals could find out if unfair information was the reason for a turndown. And it firmly recommended law-backed confidentiality "to create and define obligations with respect to the uses and disclosures that will be made of recorded information about an individual."

All well and good, and noble, too.

But like most well-meaning efforts, the study had no strong and imaginative ways to accomplish these goals. Instead, it tried to be a nice guy to everybody, including the banks, the credit card companies, the credit bureaus. Faced with the continually repeated threat that any major changes in privacy procedures and protection would be extraordinarily expensive—and that expense would be passed on to you—the study recommended avoiding unnecessary costs, by using the laws and legal powers that are already in place wherever possible and by setting up some form of reward for the information seekers-collectors if they would change their methods.

Using existing laws obviously won't work. They haven't. To expect them to improve with age or because the commission said so is to expect the days of 3% interest again. And what kind of rewards or incentives could be offered to get the banks, the credit bureaus, the data determiners to change their ways? Kewpie dolls? A new car? Free vacations? Tax breaks, perhaps, but not likely. The fact is that the information-gathering methods and systems in place today are not perfect from the bank card executive's point of view, but they are efficient and highly workable. If they weren't, the card industry wouldn't work as well as it does, wouldn't have been able to revolutionize our economy in a handful of years. To expect these people to change the system voluntarily to help you instead of themselves is to expect them to hand out 10% dscounts on your monthly billing.

The greatest hazard we face is the continual eating away of our privacy through the systematic growth and interconnecting of all of the separate record-keeping files into one totally complete record of who we are, what we've done, how we live. Our mistakes, our weaknesses, our vulnerabilities, everything but our souls, are a matter of record. And those records are part of an international grid of information-sharing computers. Any marginal official or financial service can get at them. More frightening, computer technicians and security people don't like to admit it, but they know how easy it is for unauthorized intruders to tap the network, to get into these computer files.

According to Robert Ellis Smith, publisher of *The Privacy Journal*, more than half of all labor income is now earned by people involved in the information business. More than half. The total income created by that business is more than the income made by the people who work at farming, manufacturing, or in the service industries, *combined!*

People who make a living in data processing, in telecommunications, in payrolls, in credit, in banking, are people who consistently invade your privacy. It is their job.

With that many of them out there poking, prodding, pushing

their noses into your business, your chances for privacy grow dimmer daily.

And protesting too loudly about it isn't going to help either, because that disturbance you kick up is going to end up in one of your files.

And on that great come-and-get-it day when we're all totally and completely dependent upon our card or whatever other survival device might replace it, you might finally get your privacy.

You might be left all alone without one.

11

Going for Broke

"My Visa and MasterCard are very versatile," said the middle-aged insurance-claims adjuster. "They're good for saving money at sales, good for eating out and going places, good for emergencies, but you know the thing they're really best for? Going broke."

Pick any three adults down at the bowling alley, up at the office, over on the corner, and if you have an average trio, one of them is going down the drain financially. You probably know someone like that. With a little bit of bad luck or planning, you could be that person.

Does one out of three sound high? Look at the numbers. In this country, overall, people have been using about one dollar out of every five they get to pay off debts they already owe—18–20% of their disposable personal income. That's for meals already eaten out, places already visited, suits and sofas already wearing out. But that's one of those average figures. Do you know an average person?

The truth is that as this decade started, one out of four U.S. families—or 25%—did not owe anything, so they couldn't be counted in the average figures. On top of that, 45 out of 100 owed only about one dollar out of ten—10%—to bills they'd already run up. So, roughly, 70 out of 100 families owed an average of five cents on their income dollars to paying off old bills. That left approximately one out of three people or families who owed so much they raised the whole national average to that near-20% we all theoretically owed. To accomplish that, they had to get behind 35% to 52% of their income, money that should have gone out every month to pay for last month's and even last year's buckless binges.

Edgar Allan Poe couldn't have dreamed up the horror stories that were going on.

In Los Angeles, a government employee and his working wife suddenly found themselves paying $1,100 a month to handle their outstanding credit bills. Their total combined monthly income was $1,400, which left them $300 for food, gas, rent, clothing, entertainment, and emergencies. At month's end, they were reduced to eating canned dog food, fried with eggs and grits.

In Chicago, a couple known by their neighbors as the "battling Browns" finally had their ultimate fight and separated. On the way out, Mrs. Brown took her husband's credit cards and, for spite, ran up bills of over $15,000. That was half again more than Mr. Brown brought home each year. He was more in hock than a Las Vegas crapshooter's watch. He ended up subletting their nice apartment and moving into a boarding-house, selling the family car, dressing in old clothes and eating in mission kitchens, and eventually even losing his job because of constant worry and depression.

An aircraft worker in Georgia owed so much that his teenage son was forced to quit the high-school football team to take a part-time job; his wife took in washing; his two daughters worked as store clerks after school each day and Saturdays; and the family's 1978 Oldsmobile was sold. "We eat a lot of grits and greens," he said, "and watch that TV that we still owe $400 on."

In New York, one stockbroker reported that he was so much in credit-card debt that he'd file for bankruptcy if he had the money to do it.

There are several million stories like these, and more are on the way. One writer on economic subjects says that the use of credit has been growing about twice as fast as the population and will mean twice as many debt problems. A twenty-five-year study shows that the population of the forty-eight contiguous states has gone up 41%, but bankruptcies have gone up 46%. In some depressed areas, one out of twenty-five families had to go into court, admit they lost the lifegame, and ask for official forgiveness from want, need, and the seductive, persuasive powers of open credit.

Bank card debt is not solely responsible for driving people to the courts or the poorhouse, but it is a major one. The banks control or are owed about half of all debts, including loans for cars, appliances, property improvement, personal loans, and that hard-driving debt device, the bank card.

Press releases from the financial folk bear out the debt load of bank cards:

January 30, 1979. "Worldwide dollar volume of the Visa card in the first nine months of 1978 surpassed the total for all of 1977 . . . up 49 percent."

March 30, 1979. "Visa's worldwide dollar volume rose a record 44.3% to $29.1 billion in 1978. . ."

September 13, 1979. "Visa's worldwide dollar volume rose to $8.9 billion in the quarter ended June 30, 1979, an increase of almost 30% over the corresponding period a year ago."

Although the increases were not quite so spectacular, the same thing was going on at MasterCard.

Remember, other than the early, costly setup days of the business, it had generally been high profits and unlimited growth of the bank cards. However, starting late in 1979 and running through a large part of 1980, neo-tough times hit that industry in the forms of high-cost money and increasing expenses. Most bank card departments were a bit shaky but okay. A few, which were overextended or had badly managed card programs, found themselves bleeding red ink. Overall, the card business tried to give a picture of impending disaster. Dee Hock's prediction that they would lose $1 billion on cards in 1980 was treated as stop-the-press news in daily papers. One industry publication topped his claim, said that its editor estimated the loss would run more than that. But, there are losses and there are losses.

One former card-industry executive commented, "The banks have many methods to show losses, most of them self-serving. If they wanted to show high losses for bank cards, they would say that high-cost money was going against the card program and that caused the loss. Conversely, if they wanted to show profits on the program, they would say that low-cost money was supporting the cards. In the spring of 1980, I have no doubt they put as bad a face on the situation as they could. Hock was probably counting on a 20% prime rate for all of that year. Why? To get those annual fees and higher interests they'd been wanting all along. Hock turned out to be wrong, of course, and the banks will end up making out like bandits."

While the banks weren't going under, some of their customers were. Last year alone, more than 100,000 families swallowed their pride and went to professional credit counselors, threw their hands in the air and their overdue bills on the desk. In addition to being overwhelmingly, cripplingly in debt, the great percentage of these people had other things in common.

Until the banks slowed things down in the spring of 1980, just about every debt-ridden soul in this group had been sold into spending addiction. Travel agencies were abloom with four-color posters promising exotic days and lyrical nights somewhere over the rainbow. Store-window mannequins thrust pouting lips, provocative pelvises, and preppy looks, classic looks, and California casual chic at passersby. Danish modern and distressed oak gleamed comforting, luxurious invitations from furniture-store windows. Awed, wide-eyed tots prowled miracle-filled aisles of fun-promising toys and pointed and pouted until Santa came every day of the year. Captains of elegant eateries smilingly nudged the hungry toward a la carte lobster, steaks, caviar-based sauces, pheasant-under-Steuben, and that amusingly pretentious burgundy at $35 a bottle. It was all out there, products on parade, goods going by.

All available, all yours, all now; just flash that plastic and watch the world snap to. Carefully researched slogans, backed by tens of millions of dollars in media exposure, had manipulated, urged, caressed, soothed feelings of inferiority. "Use your clout," one pushed you bravely toward the store. "Don't go anywhere without it," another one passported you to worldwide financial freedom. "We're keeping up with you," a third said, backing your every desire. Buy, consume, enjoy. Spend, and the world spends with you; save, and you save alone.

Buying on credit used to be something done by poor people

who replaced the icebox with a refrigerator—ten down, ten a month. Suddenly, according to the banks and the stores, it was the only logical, sensible, intelligent way to purchase. Thus assured by those seemingly responsible, fiscally intelligent institutions, Americans traded in their cash-and-carry training for plastic you-carry-me.

Turned loose, like a kid accidentally locked in an ice-cream store overnight, people gorged. Average credit sales in stores doubled and tripled over the amounts people would spend with cash or checks. Instead of settling for the made-in-Taiwan acrylic sweater, the cashmere from Scotland was bagged. Calvin Klein, Bill Blass, Givenchy literally walked out of the stores, on the backs of people who usually couldn't even afford the labels. Hotel presidential suites were suddenly occupied by people who ordinarily considered TraveLodge the Ritz. Château Lafite was ordered by diners who believed that *sommelier* was a country in Africa. ("Hell, waiter, only one little bottle of wine for this whole table? Bring everybody one.") Legendarily posh hotels, restaurants, stores, began appearing on everyman's bank card bill with appropriate charges. "You only live once" became "at least once a month." Bank card billings clambered upward, soared, set new records every day, week, month, quarter, year—everywhere. Only the 1980 credit controls slowed down this growth, and that effort was temporary.

What did the banks think of all of this new luxury spending, this two-Cardins-in-every-closet spree? What did they think of people who took home $1,000 a month spending that much on a weekend? How did they feel about diamond watches being bought by dime-store clerks, about Eames chairs furnishing tenements? They sent out more cards, that's how they felt. If your credit limit was $400, suddenly it was $1,000. Then you could get another card with, maybe, $1,400 on it, and still another for $1,000. You could get ten, twenty, thirty cards and up to that much in thousands of credit. One card collector, named Walter Cavanaugh, collected about a thousand of them, giving him close to $10 million worth of credit at any single time.

Journalists and psychotherapists began talking about a new national "addiction." Spendaholics and credit junkies became the names for people who went through life with plastic pressed between thumb and forefinger. Comparing them to alcoholics and to dopers was apt.

Like dope or booze, credit was used just a little at first—to get a new sense of freedom, to get a high, to obtain the beaming, beckoning good things of life they would probably otherwise never enjoy. Dope makes escape possible. Liquor makes it possible. So did bank cards.

Like dope or booze, card buying became the social thing to do. These days, a store customer who buys for cash is given the same look as a teetotaler in a bar, a straight arrow at a rock concert.

Many people, carrying an unasked-for-credit or bank card, swore they would use it only for emergencies. That was like carrying a bottle of bourbon for snakebite. Once the card was used, and the bank oh-so-leniently said that only 3–5% of what was owed on that bill had to be paid each month, plastic became intoxicating, addicting, 100 proof, straight uncut stuff. It became a big, wide, wonderful world at a common 18% annual interest.

Many began using bank cards as instant psychotherapy, solving their emotional problems by buying couches instead of renting them by the hour. (This is not exactly new. For years, well-to-do matrons found it therapeutic to get rid of the blues by getting rid of the green.)

Husbands, not as attentive to their wives because of work or mistress demands, began to make it up by purchasing flowers, jewelry, expensive dinners, and evenings out for the little woman, all on bank cards.

Aggressive upward strivers began picking up lunch, dinner, drink checks for anyone in the company who could help them get ahead.

Single working women whose lives had been controlled and dominated by an overly concerned mother and a protective father started showing their independence by repeatedly buying shouldn'ts, no-nos, and forbiddens.

The fantasy folk, the dream-world wheeler-dealers who would never be movie stars, governors, quarterbacks, or millionaires, began living like them. Cashmere sport jackets, alligator shoes, diamond cufflinks, a manicure at Tony's, and a tan from a foil-lined booth at the health club—all theirs with bank cards.

Well, if the banks weren't going to do anything about all of these driven people going into debt, what about the government? Shouldn't the government have put a stop to it all those years?

You know what the government did? It passed laws making it illegal for the banks, or any credit organization, to withhold credit because of sex, color, religion, origin, just about everything.

"But our research shows that many of these people have no credit background, or a bad one," the bankers protested.

"Sorry, it's democracy in action," the government replied.

So, additional hundreds of thousands got bank cards and used them to get away from loveless, lonely households; to escape from nine-to-five tedium; to run away from dreary, cheerless lives—even for a little while. It felt good to be out among the spenders, to be able to walk right up to a counter and buy, to be accepted as a 100% patriotic spend-for-the-economy's-sake American. It was like drinking a double martini or absorbing the kind of coke that doesn't come in bottles.

Until the hangover came in the mail. The bank was calling the marker. Not all at once, please. Just about 3% of what you owe will be fine. And 1½% of that will go for interest, which means that your debt is reduced only by the same amount.

Some card carriers figured it out. Some didn't. With payments that small, and the vigorish that high, they would be in debt to the bank for what seemed like, or actually could be, forever. Some learned. Some didn't. The didn'ts continued to use their bank cards loosely, buying things that vanished rapidly, like toothpaste, cigarettes, liquor, and lunches, having nothing to show for the money spent. Some began using two, three, four cards to buy out the stores, making a minimum payment on each card every month, letting the total amounts owed grow higher and higher. Some took out a cash advance on one card to make minimum payments on the others and then spent the balance. (Incidentally, this may be the one weakness in the entire bank card system and a fact the bankers would rather you didn't know. It is possible just about everywhere to get a cash advance with your bank card and use that money to make minimum payments on both your bank card account and on the loan. With enough cards and careful juggling of amounts, you can use the bank's money and not your own to pay off what you owe them for a very long time.)

Others, more regretful, cut up their cards, began leaving them at home or locking them away. Most of the overspenders were forced to sit back in the new month's early light and look at the wreckage they had created with their cards. A large number had been taken in by what might be considered misleading advertisements and misrepresentations by some financial institutions.

One savings-and-loan company in California ran a series of ads headlined in large black type, "IF YOU'RE HAPPY PAYING 18% INTEREST ON YOUR CREDIT CARD, DON'T APPLY FOR OURS." The second headline offered Visa and Master Charge at 12% interest, instead of the then-generally assessed 18% card rate. Way down at the bottom of the ad in telephone-directory type a disclaimer said, "Finance charges accrue from the posting of transaction to the posting of payment; this is not true of most 18% bank cards, on which finance charges do not accrue if the customer pays his entire bill each month." In other words, you pay interest on everything you buy from the day you buy it until the day you pay for it, with no "float" or free period. Individuals who signed up for that account were in for an education when the bill came in. If they decided they were misled, the savings-and-loan company merely deducted the charges and the interest from a large savings account that outfit demanded before giving out its so-called 12% card. Later, a number of other financial outfits switched to the more profitable "posting-to-payment" interest system, but at much higher rates.

There were surprises from stores, restaurants, bars, too. The Los Angeles *Times* tells of a man from Pontiac, Michigan, who stopped in a Frankfurt, West Germany, bar while he was on vacation. He said, "I had a few drinks. It was dark in there. I wasn't watching what I was signing. I thought I was paying 9.50 marks [about $5.50] for each of three drinks." It turned out to be 950 marks, and the credit card company (American Express) billed him for $1,650.70.

For those millions caught with their bills up and their income down, there was little to do but slip and slide and try to avoid the collector man. It was not easy. The banks have a great deal of experience in getting what is owed to them through highly trained collectors using time-proven techniques.

In one bank booklet, issued to individuals in a get-the-money department, there are entire sections devoted to firmly persuading people who owe money to pay it.

First, the bank breaks down the types who might be behind in payment. There is the *chronic slow pay* who "needs a nudge"; then there are the *traditional delinquent*, the *account arguers*, the *suddenly short*, and the *refuse to pays*, which the training book says "should be worked forcefully."

They've heard all of the answers, these people have. If you claim that you've already made the payment, they shoot five questions right back at you: How did you make the payment, when, how much, why didn't you make it on time, and when can you make the next one? If you broke a promise to pay, they'll crawl all over you wanting to know why you didn't pay, why the bank isn't interested in promises that aren't kept, why your credit image could be turned into a serious handicap for you. They have fast answers for other moves, too. If you're "never home," they have seven ways to find you. If you're always behind in payments, there are five firm ways to handle you.

Let's say you're sick. Here is the way a collector could talk to you:

1. Do you have accident or health insurance?
2. Any other compensation?
3. Even if somebody else in the family is sick, that's no reason not to pay us.
4. Is this illness just an excuse?
5. Why didn't you call us?

And, God forbid, you should lose your job or income:

1. You're out of work! Why? How long?
2. Do you get unemployment insurance and when are you going to send us some of it?
3. When are you going to get another job?
4. Can you borrow from friends, relatives, cash bonds, life insurance policy, savings account?
5. Do you have any back pay coming?

185

6. Is your spouse employed? Why can't he (she) make the payment?

Although it is now illegal to harass you for debts with late-night telephone calls, with notification to your employer that you're a deadbeat, with threats of emotional or physical assault, professional collectors, like military interrogators, have their ways. In the past, bill collectors, to whom the banks turn over serious delinquencies, continued to telephone incessantly, visited friends and employers to tell them you don't pay your bills, made up dunning certificates which looked like court documents, and even urged people to leave their homes by reporting a false accident of a loved one.

Once at the scene of the supposed accident, the subject was cornered by the collector and asked for money. The tougher group of bill collectors still get away with some of this because most people don't know their rights, don't know what the collectors can and cannot legally do. In some cases, the continuing pressure of the collectors leads people to emotional breakdowns, to splits with their mates, and to job loss.

There are two things you can do if you're in hock up until, let's say, March 1985 but your money will only reach to Thursday. You can go to a consumer credit counseling service. There are some two hundred of them across the nation. Recently, the average person who sought their help owed $10–12,000 and took home $1,000 a month. More than 100,000 families with money problems went to these services last year. Some heads of family were as young as nineteen. These credit counseling services are set up (1) to help with budgeting and money management, (2) to make some sense and order out of paying off the debts, and (3) to teach people how to stay away from additional debt.

The seekers fall into three groups. Two out of ten just need lessons in budgeting and money management; six out of ten need all-around help; and the remaining two are so much in debt that not even professionally trained counselors can help.

They see them all:

One counselor in New York talked to a man who was spending $397 a day more than he earned.

A New York doctor whose income was $200,000 a year owed more than $160,000.

At a California office, three CPA's came in for financial help.

At another one, a university professor confessed that he owed the equivalent of his next two years' salary. When the counselor totaled up the bills, it turned out to be even more.

One of the first things the credit counselors do is castrate credit by cutting up your credit cards then and there. As the counselor's scissors cut the credit card, overspenders have been known to turn pale, let out involuntary cries of "Oh no!" grow faint, and even go into a form of temporary shock. Learning to live without bank card credit, for some, is like learning to live without a leg, or an arm, or a dear loved one.

Especially hard hit are the multiple card carriers. There is a popular but totally incorrect belief that the more bank cards a person has, the better is his or her credit. However, credit card counselors point out that multiple cards can easily lead to multiple debts because card users tend to use two, three, four of them to run up two, three, four times the debt which would be permitted on only one card. Too, bankers consider credit card lines of credit as debts, *whether they are used or not*. Bankers know that you can use that credit at any time, so tend to tighten up on any other type of borrowing you might want to do.

Facing destruction of their plastic passports to purchasing paradise, some card carriers still show the credit counselors who's boss. They will deliberately lie about how many cards they have (and some have four dozen) or leave some home. Others will just go out and reapply for new cards after the counselor destroys the existing ones. Even when the tighter credit restrictions came along, many banks continued profligate issuing of cards.

After the credit circumcision, heavy debtors are put on a very strict budget, which allows enough for food, transportation, rent, utilities. The rest of incoming money then goes to the counseling service, which divides it up, pays each creditor an amount toward outstanding bills. The creditors, the people owed, are contacted earlier and asked if they'll accept payment that way. Some 99% of them do.

The director of one California counseling service said, "There is no doubt that credit [bank] cards are responsible for the great increase in debt. We send more money to the Bank of America than to anyone else. There are very few accounts we handle that didn't come in with anywhere from 2 to 8 Visa and Master Charge cards. One came in with 30.

"Citibank [of New York] solicited nearly everyone on the West Coast. Everyone coming in here has a Citibank card, and apparently they were issued without looking at people's ability to pay."

High-gambling Citibank, the snappy spender of the industry, was answered by California's local banks. They sent out whatever card their best customers didn't have, making Visa carriers into Master Charge users and vice versa. Individuals who had a Visa with one bank and a Master Charge with another now had both from each bank, and until late 1979, other banks around the state and the country were deluging them with offers for more.

The trouble with bank cards, according to that counselor, is that the banks then asked for only 3% or 4% of the money due as a monthly payment. "They want those accounts overdue. They even send bills which tell you how much money you haven't spent out of your credit limit, encouraging you to spend even more." Many banks raised this minimum during the credit crisis, but some went up only 1% or 2% a month.

Ironically, most of the funds to keep these counseling services running come from the institutions which are owed the money. The counseling centers ask them to volunteer a 15% rebate for every dollar they get an overdue customer to pay. Other income stems from employer, foundation, or union contributions, and even small charges made to the people in trouble, if they can afford it. In one recent year, the National Foundation for Consumer Credit had a banker as past chairman of the board, two bankers on the executive committee, and three on the board of trustees. Bankers, in general, are sympathetic to the plan. Most feel that this way they will get their money and that the 15% cost could easily be less than the cost of collection agencies or taking people to court. As more and more people fell behind in payment, these services became increasingly important.

Do they work? About half and half. During 1979, somewhere between 50% and 65% of the people who came in for help stayed with the program and worked out their debts. Some decided to work it off themselves. Others went back to their own personal law of economics: Gimme, but don't ask for none. A few of the debt-ridden had tried those much-advertised "debt-consolidation services," which are now illegal in many states. What they got were very high interest rates from cunning lenders and interminably extended or backbreaking payments to replace shorter-term and smaller ones.

The other way to go straight while going broke is bankruptcy. According to admittedly incomplete reports in mid-1979, there were 14% more personal bankruptcies filed in the United States than the year before and an overall increase of close to 25% since 1971, the real birthing year of the bank card swarm. Bankruptcy isn't what it used to be. At one time saying you couldn't pay your bills was worse than the wearing of a scarlet A for a girl or being called a pansy for a boy. Today, scarlet women, pansies, and bankruptcy are all integral parts of our society and attract less attention than holes in a construction-site fence. In fact, once bankruptcy is declared, it can't be done again for another six years. People who want to lend you money know that and also know that you can't stiff them again for a while, so they'll offer you more credit. There have been cases of people declared bankrupt who immediately received shiny new credit cards from stores to which they already owed hundreds of dollars that would never be paid.

There have been two traditional ways to file for bankruptcy. One is called Chapter 13 of the Federal Bankruptcy Act. A federal court tells you how much to pay, then distributes that money to your creditors on an extended repayment plan. It works like a credit counseling service except that the word "bankruptcy" is attached to it.

The other choice is a straight bankruptcy, in which a trustee appointed by the court takes over most of what you own, sells it, and gives the money to the creditors. Once that's done, you owe no man, even if your assets paid off only a little of the debt.

What you can keep depends on where you live. In one state, you can keep a house if you don't have too much equity in it, but in another they'll take your house, car, television, everything, leaving you with a small amount of clothing and personal items. A third state seems to be the place. There, in most cases, you can keep your personal belongings, your car, and your house, regardless of how much value they have. (Obviously the thing to do there in case of impending bankruptcy is put your money into a ranch and a Rolls Royce.)

Because of our basic training in the American virtues of solidity and good financial standing, and because of long-standing fears of collectors, most of us want to pay our bills and to become responsible budgeters and financial managers. No one has yet isolated a national genetic defect which motivates us to get into deep debt and to disregard, walk away from, or cheat to get out of it. Overspending is a habit we've been taught, not one we inherited.

Perhaps the dilemma was best summed up by a stock clerk named Joseph Schwartz of San Francisco, who went $4,000 into the credit card hole before a psychiatrist and credit counselors helped him curb debt addiction. "I don't believe in ripping people off," he said, "but the common man needs a taste of the good life, too."

Well, with all of those goodies out there and all of that plasticapability to buy them inside our pockets, how's a person to stay out of heavy debt?

Here are a few thoughts for the day:

1. Don't think about what you're doing. Barge right in and buy that charming new dress, that theater ticket, those record albums. Just because you don't need a new dress, you read bad reviews of the show, and you hate music shouldn't deprive you of spending joy. On the other hand, what would happen if you did give some long consideration to what you were buying before you used your bank card?

2. Eliminate all copies of sales slips, statements, receipts from your bank card purchases. Throw them away immediately. That way you won't be reminded of how much you spent, and your statement will be a big surprise. Or, what would happen if you stuck them all up on the bathroom mirror and had to look at them several times a day?

3. Balk at putting a personal credit limit on your spending. It's your salary, isn't it? And you worked for it, so you deserve the best and you deserve it now. Why should you limit your credit spending to a handle-able 10% or even a manageable 15%? Besides, you like spaghetti at month's end and the landlord is fairly patient about the rent, right?

4. Take and use the first bank card that comes to hand. They're all the same, aren't they? Blue-white-gold is Visa; the one with the circles is MasterCard. What's the difference which bank it comes from? There couldn't be any differences in charges, fees, and how they figure their interest rates, could there? Have you ever checked to find out, especially with all the recent changes?

Notice that the first letters of each section spell out DEBT, and that's where you're headed, living by these rules.

Too much credit can be a problem with companies, too. Just like you, if a company owes more than it can handle, it could go under. It doesn't happen only to small firms. According to the Los Angeles *Times*, in 1978 the largest retailing operation in the world, Sears Roebuck & Co., chose to sell $550 million worth of credit its customers owed that company to a group of sixteen banks. Some of the money received was used to pay off companies that had sold goods to Sears. J. C. Penney elected to follow that path in early 1980 when it planned to sell $260 million (later up to $350 million) of outstandings to a subsidiary of New York's enterprising Citicorp, among others. The reason these companies had to sell and discount this money was that their own credit card customers weren't paying soon enough or fast enough to keep things on a good economic plane.

These days, government officials and bank spokesmen preen themselves by saying that credit use is being cut back, that people are getting frightened of debt, are learning to handle their credit cards, and that the 1980 temporary credit controls worked.

It isn't that simple. Despite a temporary slowdown, people were not giving up their bank cards. Visa and MasterCard volume figures prove that. Ted Wooton, Bank of America's Southern California manager for charge cards, gave out figures to the Los Angeles *Times* which indicate that some economic experts are out to lunch. BankAmericard Visa spending was up 25% for 1979 and continued with great strength into early 1980. Worldwide, Visa's gross dollar volume was up over 30% for 1979 over 1978, Interbank's was up close to 28%. The credit cutbacks of 1980 were but a pause for second wind by the running-to-ruin credit card spenders.

What did fall off was other credit spending. People weren't

buying toys anymore. Mobile homes, recreation vehicles, trail motorcycles, and other impractical playthings were being passed by in these petroleum-poor days. When tough days finally hit the credit business, the bankers used that "crisis" as an excuse to more tightly control customer lists. Some banks and department stores started turning down anywhere from 40 to 60% of new credit applications (while, conversely, others continued to increase their bank card lists). Their qualifications were made tougher, yes, but most new applications were from not particularly good credit risks. The good ones already had cards; saturation of the country's creditworthies was nearly total.

The Los Angeles *Times* quotes House Majority Leader James Wright of Texas, alarmed about all this, as saying, "We've got to get rid of the credit-card economy to some degree. . . ." Sorry, Mr. Wright, but it's too late. While no one was really watching the door, bank cards came in, cash and currency were swept out. Get rid of credit, especially the bank cards? One large retailer said, "Without bank cards we'd lose from one-third to one-half of our sales of luxury, expensive, and profitable items. We'd go out of business." Instead of being just a nice convenience extended to a few choice customers (which was the original idea of credit cards), the sale is wagging the dog. Most of the retail world has become just as hooked on credit selling as its customers are on credit buying.

Wild-spending shoppers used to be the gossip of the employees' lounge. Then they became common, as common as their cards. One representative customer of that type reported, "Look at me. I have a walk-in closet that won't hold another coathanger. I can't walk into it anyhow because the floor is covered with shoes. I give away clothes I haven't even worn." Did that confession come from an heiress, a billionaire's wife, a movie star? Not at all. The lady talking was Jeanne Fioretto, a "modestly salaried" editor of a professional journal. So distressed did she become with her uncontrollable card spending that she finally organized a group called Overspenders Anonymous in Wisconsin. It was similar in operation to Debtors Anonymous in New York and Alcoholics Anonymous and Gamblers Anonymous just about everywhere. When a member was in a store and fingers were trembling, not for a drink or a pair of dice, but for a pencil to sign a charge slip, that person could call for help. Someone showed up and talked him out of the purchase. The founder of Overspenders Anonymous probably wishes there had been a discouraging friend nearby when she made one of her purchases. "I bought an outboard motorboat. Can you imagine? I don't need a boat, don't want a boat, and I bought a boat."

Boats, fur coats, jewelry, truffle sauces, and Dom Perignon are some of the many luxuries people can live without and which are bought with bank cards. Card carriers can buy skis, a vacation in a nudist camp, birth-control counseling, videotape players, an appendectomy for the dog, and a nose job for its master. That's what people are buying, so that's what others are selling. Our children are growing up, not with images of Benjamin Franklin's thrift, or Lincoln's walk to return extra change, but with memories of Mommy looting the department-store racks and Daddy buying enough ski gear to outfit the Austrian downhill team.

Nobody, especially not the bankers, has suggested that maybe part of the tens of billions spent on luxuries every year should go into cleaning up our ghettos, cutting medical costs, purifying our air, developing mass transportation, and strengthening our educational system. Like Mommy. Like Daddy. Tomorrow will be like today, but more so. Do you have it in a size twelve? Waiter, bring the biggest steak in the house. Two seats on the Concorde, please.

The unofficial but legendary Marine Corps motto has come true.

Screw you, Mac. I got mine.

My Visa. My MasterCard. My debt.

And for some, my bankruptcy. The reason we allow bankruptcies in this country is that the law says a person can not be jailed for debts. But there are no laws which offer a God-given or constitutionally derived right to credit or to credit cards, especially if you've proven you can't handle them.

Even if you've gone in over your head just trying to survive, not from buying luxuries, there will still be no excuse.

When it all comes together, if you've been chronically

delinquent in payments, have had to turn your financial management over to credit counselors, or have filed bankruptcy, you are going to be SOL.

Shut Out of Lifebank.

There are over 16 million people who can't get credit today, who won't be able to qualify for Lifebank tomorrow.

Keep spending wildly with your cards. You can make it 16 million and one.

12

Sharing

"If LIVING OFF of bank cards is the American Way, then we must be true patriots. We're going as broke as the Liberty Bell."

Quick, who said that: (A) Head of a family which is ninety days behind in card payments, (B) Operator of a check-cashing service, (C) Owner of a coin-vending-machine route, (D) A banker?

If you guessed A, B, or C, you get a D. If you guessed D, you get an A. If you're a small-time or inefficient banker, you knew it all along.

Although the great majority of banks have found "solid gold," not all of them are benefiting from the Big Bank Card Bonanza, especially lately. Some are facing increasing financial problems because of their card programs, some are going into heavy debt because of their card programs, and in the larger view, all card-carrying banks might face tragic consequences for them and for us because of those card programs. The problems are not all limited to the economy, either.

Take the small-time banks, banks with limited card activity or banks in small towns or outlying suburbs. Most of them are cashing in handsomely with cards. Visa's U.S. institutions, which did up to $60 million a year in card volume, were averaging out three to four times the net-profit percentage of their bigger brothers, which did over $240 million a year, according to one 1979 quarterly study. You'd think that everything was okay in River City or Commutertown, but it isn't. Quite a few of the small banks are having big problems, and they are being compounded daily.

One of their major difficulties is turf. They don't control it anymore. There was a time when First Hometown Bank and maybe one or two same-sized competitors had the financial franchise for the area. Today, slick, fast-moving, aggressive banks from out of the area and even out of the state have moved in with their big-city palaver and their electronic medicine shows to amaze and dazzle the local populace.

For example, Citicorp, which owns and runs New York's hard-running Citibank, has been looking for greener pastures, geographically and financially. For general banking, that organization has opened out-of-state offices to compete with their local brethren for corporate business, leasing, lending, for financial-counseling services and other money-making pursuits. Citibank is just one long-armed bank; there are plenty of others. Although laws prohibit or restrict branch banking outside of an institution's home state, certain activities are excepted. The exceptions are becoming the rule.

One of Citibank's most defiant moves was the recruitment of cardholders from an estimated twenty-five states outside of New York. A federal law says that banks can't blindly mail unsolicited cards anymore, that people must ask for them. Making an end run around that rule, Citibank sent out a mass mailing of "reservation" forms which were cleverly constructed to get more card carriers into the Citibank data bank and profit columns. The letters were masterpieces of direct-mail-selling techniques, included phrases like "Because of your excellent credit standing," and "No application needed," and "You must act by March 31 to be eligible," and "Process immediately."

One Citibank letter offered a new card to its receivers, even though many of them already had that card from a local bank. By giving citizens a second card, Citibank could cut in on local card spending, which cut down on local bank profits. Citibank's conduct was considered greedy and arrogant by other bankers. They complained that Citibank didn't really care how much their conduct might contribute to the debt-and-delinquency problems of consumers and the nation or the millions in fraud losses that might come out of a mailing like that. Some small local banks were hard hit by that mailing's consequences. So was Citibank. Of the estimated 5 million people who accepted the card offer, many turned out to be bad risks. Citibank is still financially shaken by that experience.

In addition, the new electronic hookups were webbing in our distant outposts, our remote villages, our long-drive suburbs, into one credit-controlled community. Small banks, which do not have much electronic machinery or the financial capital to buy it, were losing business to the new money systems. The cash machine on the corner, the automatic teller down the street, could belong to a bank upstate, downstate, or even out of state.

In those states where branch banking was allowed, street corners, supermarket walls, and shopping-center malls carried these electronic outposts for institutions hundreds, even a thousand or more miles away. In states where branch banking is illegal, these facilities were not considered branches, as such. In both cases, Larry and Linda Local could help themselves to big-city banking right on the town square, from the terminal guarded by a moldy bronze Civil War soldier.

All Larry and Linda knew was that the machine helped with banking and didn't have bad breath. There was no warning sign which told them their business was going out of the area and affecting the performance and solidity of First Hometown Bank. The final score was Visitors 1, Hometown 0. Larry and Linda Local ran into this situation again in the local clothing emporium. Using their First Gotham instead of their First Hometown card in a point-of-sale terminal, they bypassed the local financial group and pledged their debt and its interest to high-flying bankers in a high-rise building many miles away.

Through all of these transactions, First Hometown Bank had lost the merchant kickbacks, the interest on bank card debt, the interest on cash advances. Today, there is much banker discussion about "sharing," a system in which Linda and Larry could use First Gotham Bank's electronic terminals with either their out-of-state or their local card. To date, sharing is something done by schoolchildren and encounter groups but not by many bankers. "Why should we allow the local bank to make money on the expensive lash-up we installed, and if so,

197

how much?" ask the giants. "Even if we could afford it, how many cash machines and automated tellers can one town handle, and where is the break-even for all of the banking industry?" ask the local banks. This problem is not settled. It is the third crease from the top in bank card executives' furrowed brows.

This draining of commercial and card business from local banks by better-capitalized, faster-moving, more aggressive outsiders is causing many small banks to look at the pros and cons of their card business and to hope they balance out . . . on the balance sheet. One solution which Citicorp, parent of Citibank, has developed is a program which would enlist small banks in a national network tied together with those automated teller machines. To many rural bankers that would be like letting the horses into the cornfield.

"Sharing" is but a small problem in banking these days. There are much bigger ones which could affect their, and our, total economic security.

One of the most frightening is the total lack of traditional bank financial security which the bank card business has created. If bankers were selling hundred-dollar bills for a buck, that still wouldn't be as fiscally irresponsible as what they're doing with the bank cards. These days, if a customer goes into a bank to borrow money for an automobile, an appliance, property improvement, mobile home, or to get teeth fixed, the bank will ask for security on that loan. They want some form of collateral to make sure that loan is secured. Yet, those same customers, with multiple bank cards, can "borrow" up to $15,000 without putting up their firstborn, Krugerrands, General Motors stock, the old homestead, or cent one. All it takes is a good credit rating and a signature. This "soft" paper—or unprotected, unsecured loan—is based simply on the bank's expectation of repayment. If that card loan isn't repaid, the bank has no car to sell, no stocks to cash in, no gold to put against the debt. That good credit rating isn't even negotiable anymore, because it just turned bad. Getting the money back becomes time-consuming, difficult, and expensive for the bank. The end result could be a potentially crippling washout or a charge-off.

198

The difference between a recession and a depression is that during a recession you have to tighten your belt and during a depression you have no belt to tighten. When those blights land on us, many people are unemployed because others are not buying what these people build or sell. That has been happening in the housing and the automobile and other industries recently. Without a job, those individuals do not have an income and are not able to pay their bank-card installments. *The Nilson Report* said that the 1979 average amount of money owed by bank card users was $480.46 for Master Charge users and $501.39 for Visa spenders. Other sources say those balances are much higher. The total amount of credit on bank cards owed domestically at the end of 1979 was over $25 billion in charges and close to $30 billion including cash advances. That was $25 billion the banks had outstanding. It was unsecured by anything but the banks' belief that it would be paid back.

But the bank card bill is only one debt. Most Americans have others, too, and are in hock up to their wallet stitching. In March 1979, every adult and child in the nation owed $5.6 thousand. At the end of 1978, our households owed 83.3% of what was left after taxes. Much of this debt is in secured, or "hard," paper. There are homes, automobiles, stocks, cattle, other "hard" goods which the banks can grab to handle unpaid loans. Do you believe that people are going to pay their Visa card bill before their home mortgage, their MasterCard statement before their car payment? According to Don Quixote, a good name may be better than riches, but he was riding around on a nag, didn't need a car to look for a job.

The banks cannot afford much of an interruption in repayment activity, especially in the card business. They no longer have the kind of capital reserves they used to keep. Their capital-to-loans ratios have been way down. Even the early 1980 Federal Reserve Board requirements that strengthened them were still too little, too late.

In the recent past, bank executives have cut heavily into reserves to make somewhat risky investments in electronic banking, to put up architectural wonders as home offices, to give top executives the type of incomes enjoyed by movie

199

producers and narcotics importers. One economic forecasting company announced that banks were loaning out some 70% of deposits in 1976, but 83% in 1979.

For a considerable period, new money, the traditional deposits banks count on to keep going, was not coming in very rapidly. Only the lazy, the compulsively conservative, the unconscious, and the dumb were putting their money into low-interest-paying savings accounts. With 12%, 13%, 14% interest out there on T-bills or T-bill bank accounts, people were lined up during the bank working day, shifting their money from low savings-account interest to a rate of return closer to today's money-eating inflation. As a result, the banks had less low-interest money to put behind the cards.

In addition, the banks had to pay out higher interest rates on increasingly more money. They were in a trash-compactor squeeze. At some points, what the banks were paying for outside money started to endanger the card programs and their overall economic health. One-third of the card users were still paying their bills on time and paying no interest at all, so the banks were losing money on them. They also lost interest during the float, or free, period while the money was lent out but no interest was owed. Bankers considered that float period a 1–2% loss all by itself. Too, not all bank-card money was lent out at 18% interest. Some banks charged 18% only on the first $500 or $1,000 and then the scale went down to 12% for the amount which was owed over that. Starting in mid-1980, however, where legal, many banks went to a set interest percentage on everything owed.

Very costly card delinquencies and fraud cut heavily into capital, too. Bankers don't like to talk about these areas, because they show that the card system has holes in it. Losses by fraud and losses due to people who don't pay up are kept quieter than a library reading room, but they're as dangerous to the banks as a gang of Willie Suttons.

As far back as the first quarter of 1979, Visa alone admitted fraud losses of $1.66 for each thousand dollars of business it did. Since it did close to $10 billion, worldwide, for that time period, the loss would be $16.6 million for the quarter; and at that rate, approximately $66.4 million for the year. Master-

Card's figures were somewhat similar, so double that to over $130 million which the bankers lost that year to fraud alone and which had to be written off. Newsletter publisher Nilson says that the banks are pulling our legs, that those fraud losses are really running over $1 billion a year and are increasing heavily.

Add to that the credit write-offs, the bills which will never be paid. For the same calendar quarter, Visa was charging off $8.44 for every thousand dollars' worth of business, writing it off because it wasn't collectible. That's more than five times the amount being lost by fraud; close to $400 million a year. And Master Charge was running similar figures. One estimate says the bank cards are losing over $25 million a week now. Both fraud and write-off losses combined were causing a shortage of red Bics in bank office-supply closets.

Nilson also predicted that U.S. bank-card losses from unpaid bills and fraud would run close to $3 billion a year by 1985. Depending upon economic conditions, that figure could be more conservative than wingtip cordovans.

There are other holes in the money bucket. Running a card program is not cheap. It takes salaries, employee benefits, data-processing equipment and maintenance, floor space, advertising, postage, furniture, supplies, outside processing, credit reports, interchange fees paid to other banks, and other essentials. One card system is bad enough. Most banks have two—Visa and MasterCard. Because they might run afoul of the antitrust laws by handling them together, most banks run them like fraternal twins, and that almost doubles the costs. Today, many banks are reviewing the doubtful blessings of this double system.

Banks have major problems in other departments, too. International currency fluctuations, investments in Eurodollars, real-estate trusts which have gone sour, bad debts on housing and automobile industry transactions, large long-term loans out at low interest rates, are a few of them. All take their toll of bank solidity. The Federal Deposit Insurance Corporation admitted in late 1980 that it had a list of over 250 "problem" banks, some of them very sizable institutions. Dangers which could cripple many banks include increased prices for imported oil, speculative surges in commodities and other markets, the recession spreading overseas, continuing trouble with the domestic automobile industry.

One of the crucial problems in bank solidity is the bank card. Appearing more and more at bank card conferences and conventions are speeches or seminars on "Cutting Credit Costs," "Reducing Fraud and Delinquencies," and "Making Money with Your Card Programs." One banker who attends these meetings regularly commented, "I go, hoping somebody there can teach me how to get my outs in."

Before you get too sympathetic and want to send a get-well card to the banks, think about how all of this financial roughness can lead to outright disaster for you, too.

Add it up.

Bank Cards:

1. Smaller banks are facing increasingly destructive competition from the larger ones.

2. Large investments in electronic funds transfer systems are not yet paying off.

3. Fraud and delinquency losses are mounting.

4. The cost of money is fluctuating for the banks.

5. For a while, banks were limited to a 6–9% maximum growth on unsecured credit activities.

6. Banks must carry duplicate expenses for two card systems.

7. Card "loans" are in "soft," or unsecured, paper.

General Banking:

8. Salaries and overhead are going up.

9. Many banks do not have strong reserves. Some banks are so capital-poor they chose to drop out of the Federal Reserve System rather than try to meet the Fed's demands for solidity. However, even nonmembers had to meet the Fed's new bank-strengthening rules.

10. Many banks have heavy chunks of money tied up in bad or low-paying long-term investments which do not return today's higher interest.

11. Problems with petrodollars, Eurodollars, and unstable international currency exchange have hit some banks.

12. Bad investments in real estate, housing, automotive industry are taking their toll.

13. Many economists say that most importantly, banks could be in major trouble because of petroleum debts.

Because of these and other reasons, many banks are living on borrowed time instead of borrowed money.

When the 1980 re(de)pression arrived, there were two more card-originated drains helping to suck the banks dry. Card carriers began slowing down bill payments but continued to use their cards to survive. Faced with widespread activity of this type, the banks were running weeks, even months, behind trying to cut off these people, trying to get this runaway unpaid spending stopped. It is easy to stop a thousand people who overspend with the card and who do not keep up payments, but what does a bank do if 50,000, 250,000, a half-million card carriers do it all at once? On top of that, those same people and their friends were shutting down their savings accounts, not renewing their T-bill accounts, and using up their checking accounts just to get along. Money the bank was counting on to operate kept walking out the door.

One night that door could be locked and it might not open the next morning—(drawn) shades of the 1930's!

If some banks start to go belly-up, you and your friends will probably stampede financial institutions to get your money before those organizations, too, do an el foldo. The banks will not have the cash available to pay you off. It is very possible they will not even be able to raise it because a very high percentage of deposits are invested elsewhere. Too, many of their old investments were made at lower interest rates and are not too readily salable today. Because the money owed on bank cards is unbacked by anything, the market for "soft" paper will also be soft. Faced with demands for your money and the inability to raise it, many banks might close, forever.

This is not supposed to happen. Theoretically, the Federal Deposit Insurance Corporation will refund your money if the bank doesn't have it. The FDIC was put together to make sure of that. The idea may be sound, but the finances are not. The FDIC cannot cover the losses created by multiple bank failures in a short time. It does not have the money. There was more than $335,000,000,000 ($335 billion) in non-governmental commercial bank checking accounts in this country at the end of

1979. The FDIC, by using its own funds, by borrowing from the Treasury, and by selling off the broken bank's assets, raises the money to repay you. By the end of 1979, that organization had only $10 billion to cover losses, plus another $3 billion it could borrow through Congress.

If just one very large bank went under, the FDIC would be as broke as you are, and just about as helpless to do anything about the problem.

So, we are not alone. Because of some unsound banking practices, including the unsecured bank card, the banks could also be in big trouble. The bank card could be the critical weak spot which undermines banking stability.

In addition to the banks, the entire economic system of the United States could be in peril partially because of the heavy impact of credit and bank card spending in helping to create inflation.

Inflation is more money chasing the same or fewer goods and services. The "money" you spend with a bank card is not sitting around in your savings and checking accounts or in your wallet. It is credit, borrowed against future earnings. It actually creates a new pool of spending power. As was mentioned earlier, in one recent year the Federal Reserve authorized the printing and distribution of $10 billion in new currency. At the same time, the bank cards upped credit possibilities over $11 billion to people who already had cards. That was 10% more than the amount of "new money" being put out there by the government. Totally, the amount of new bank card credit, to new and old users, went up over $16 billion between 1978 and 1979. Both the new currency and the new credit were unbacked or unsecured by anything of material value. The major difference is that currency is controlled by the Fed, but up until mid-1980, there was no real operational control or authority over credit.

The banks did not control it. They issued it, processed it, made money on it, but did not control it. This is why: When you buy something with a card, the store sends a slip for that sale to the bank so it can get paid. That payment, minus the bank's kickback, is put into that store's account. You have, basically, been issued a small loan from the bank. The amount you spent has been paid by the bank to the store. (Bankers are beginning to argue that this is not a "loan," but a service, so that they can maneuver fees and charges, legally.) You have spent new money. Because you did not use the money in your checking or savings account, you didn't reduce the amount of money around or recirculate that money. So, essentially, credit and bank cards create more purchasing power, and that is one of the prime causes of inflation.

While all of this was going on, while bank card carriers were being given tens and tens of billions of unsecured spending power every year, the Federal Reserve Board sat by and did nothing. Only when government figures showed that inflation was running nationally at an 18% annual rate did it come off the bench with some new signals. The problem was, the game was nearly over and our side was losing badly. Putting restrictions on bank cards was like tackling the right guard while the tailback was off and running with the ball.

Following the credit controls announced by the Fed in early 1980, a squad of professional economists was agreed that the action was meant purely as a crowd pleaser and that it wasn't nearly thorough enough, comprehensive enough, or tough enough to solve the nation's economic problems. One longtime financial observer pointed out that the Fed had done absolutely nothing about the close-to-70% of bank card credit which was still out there available to Visa and MasterCard wielders. The concept of credit control and a sane policy to control consumer overspending vanished operationally and officially by fall 1980.

This now-continuing inflationary, uncontrolled, bank-busting problem is so large it is not even limited to the United States. Like Coca-Cola, we are exporting it.

One of Visa's executives recently said the world became ". . . a global village, trading in cruzerios and krone, pesetas and pounds, in yen, rupee, drachma, franc, lira, quetzal, won, and baht," all through the common denominator of the bank card. At the same time, Interbank was working to strengthen an already established international system which differs from Visa's only because it doesn't demand a one-world/one-card identification system.

With virtual card saturation of the profitable United States population, Visa's leaders began to exploit the remainder of the world. The figures were more attractive than a Las Vegas chorus line's. In late 1979, only a little more than 31% of Europe's solid citizens were carrying charge cards, compared to some 90% here, and they carried only 1.4 cards compared to 7.6 in the U.S. In addition, Europe has some 124 million eligible card customers, compared to some 85 million domestically.

By 1980 the far-flung Visa empire had colonized more than 135 countries. Banks from Paraguay, Ireland, Thailand, Spain, Kuwait, Chile, Sweden, Ecuador, Pakistan, Luxembourg, Israel, Argentina, Mexico, Italy, Kenya—just about everywhere things were bought and sold—were part of the Visa network. Only telephone companies connected more countries than the Visa system. In one year, 1,000 institutions joined up. The tri-striped card was more popular and more recognizable overseas than a Clint Eastwood film. By the beginning of 1980, sales volume reached about $10 billion, U.S. The growth continues. Visa's overseas experts expected sales on that card to go up another 50% during 1980. MasterCard's 1979 out-of-country activities ran some $7 billion and its aggressive new overseas growth plans promised dramatic increases within the next few years.

Some European financial organizations were alarmed at the rapidity and thoroughness with which the American bank card systems moved into their areas. One unsigned paper which was passed around to European banks warned about the "expansionist airs of the American mass credit card Visa, due to the complete saturation of the American market and problems of profitability . . ." and ". . . the efforts being made by American credit card organizations to corner the European market and dismantle the cheque card system, to replace it with credit cards under American control."

Dee Hock had tried resolutely to head off this type of attack. In a long speech delivered to the European Financial Marketing Association in early 1979, he attempted to assure the international banking community that Visa was not pushing for a single way to exchange value; that it wanted to give each bank the freedom to operate the way it chose; that Visa would never compete with its members, that it would cooperate with them.

However, in the same speech, he also emphasized the need for common standards and for one worldwide communication system for the exchange of value. Moving toward the one-world/one-card idea, he said that Visa was not a credit card organization and was not American; that Europeans owned and developed the Visa business on that continent; and that the Visa board was multinational.

At one point he outlined the basic structure of what was being shaped up as Lifebank. "If one views the world as a whole," he said, "it is apparent that the consumer may place his earnings in the custody of financial institutions in many forms. We shall refer to these as reservoirs of value, which the customer is constantly replenishing with payments or deposits. A reservoir of value may be a checking account, a savings account, an investment handled by a trust department, a fund-raising from sale of travelers cheques, or a line of credit against future earnings. The reservoirs of any one consumer may be in a single institution or in several. The traditional means of access, such as passbooks and checks, have been operationally and geographically limited."

What he was describing was the basic framework of Life-bank, in which all of your value would be in a "reservoir" and in which savings-account passbooks and checkbooks won't work. What was needed, obviously, was something like a financial transaction or Lifebank card to make it operational for you and for the bankers.

Not everyone struck his colors for the Visa stripes. Countries in Central Europe, already heavily invested and involved in existing systems called Eurocard and Eurocheck, said no. Germany, Austria, Belgium, and Holland accepted something called visas at their borders, but not within their banks. During 1980, MasterCard executives began to rebuild that card's international strength by tying in with those strong European groups.

In answer, Bank of America-Visa decided to open its own card center in West Germany during the fall of 1979. From that location, the plan was to bring Central Europe the enlightenment of Visa's money missionaries.

Like an electric appliance, the Visa card did not work as well in some foreign countries as in others. In some of the 135 Visa-associated countries, you couldn't check out of a hotel after an extended stay before eight o'clock in the morning; couldn't buy dinner for a large party at ten P.M. in fourteen countries; couldn't escape all of that by purchasing an airline ticket on Sunday in more than fifteen countries. The problem was downtime for the Visa authorization centers. They were closed at those hours, and you couldn't get your card and credit cleared.

Visa's electronic troops got busier than telephone linemen after a tornado. By mid-1979 they had hooked up the domestic BASE I credit-clearing system directly with Europe, had expended an autotelex system to service far-flung countries from the Caribbean to Asia, had added a new mini-computer program to handle countries with smaller communications needs. Throughout the world, some 30,000 terminals were tied in to the system, and 25% more were scheduled for addition every year.

Visa officials optimistically counted on 1980 to show $50 billion spent with its card and new traveler's check program through more than 100 million cards throughout the world. The more distant future looked even better: a projected worldwide sales volume of $180 billion just a few years away, and just for Visa alone.

As the American bank card systems colonized the world's countries, the American Express card grew a little greener, especially around the gills. Long the leader for overseas spending by Americans, and original franchise holder for internationally recognized credit, it began losing heavily to Visa and MasterCard. There was $69 billion spent with the two bank cards and American Express in 1978. Visa had 42% of that spending, MasterCard had 40%, American Express slipped from 20% to 18% in that year alone, and its executives could see a continuing downward slide ahead.

By late 1979, Visa alone had 12,000 financial institutions with close to 74,000 offices throughout the world, all wired in to that organization. With that kind of base, one-world/one-card/one-system became increasingly more possible. With terminals increasing like summer tourists, with lines and cables and wires tying 135 or more countries into the common Visa system, with one set of standards and operating procedures, with many of the world's major bankers agreed on the need to switch from credit cards to transaction or financial cards, Lifebank was becoming increasingly more realistic.

Along with the blessings of basketball, Levi's, bourbon, jazz, and UCLA sweatshirts, the world was getting the blessings of American bank card systems. In trying to provide the citizens of our globe with "unrestricted 24-hour access to their value," the bank card groups also included—at no extra charge—advantages of possible debt addiction, overspending, invasion of privacy, loss by fraud and theft, and reduction of identity to a number, all in one made-in-the-USA high-impact-plastic package.

From First Hometown Bank to First Gotham Bank, the financial people are not worried about those problems; they are worried about banking problems. They are concerned that expensive EFT systems are not paying off yet, that delinquencies and fraud are running into unmanageable figures, that bank card profits have been down, that inter-system competition is hurting some smaller banks, that "soft"-paper bank card outstandings make them vulnerable. Too, the bank and bank-selected entities which have had total control of the bank card business faced new and aggressive competition for card business when the federally chartered savings-and-loans began Visa and MasterCard programs in 1980. Not all of these problems could be solved by the transaction-card-operated Lifebank system, but many of them could. That is why many leaders of the Visa and MasterCard systems have chosen to move outward and onward, to recruit the entire world into the ultimate Lifebank system. At no time in history have so many of the world's bankers been so sold, so dedicated, so organized, so uniformly oriented to one type of banking service with one set of standards and operating procedures, and one determined goal.

The world's banks are looking to Visa and MasterCard to share the ways to more profitable, more organized, and more controlling card activities. They are looking to those companies for the financial version of making atomic energy.

But worldwide exporting of the way the bank-card business is run here—without remedying the defects first—is, instead, more like sharing the know-how for making atomic waste.

13

Out of Control

EARLY BANKAMERICARD ADVERTISEMENTS urged us to think of it as money.

Later messages continued to manipulate logic by assuring us the bank card was just our old friend money in a new, more convenient form.

The bankers know better than that. Or they should be fired for not understanding basic economics.

The bank card is not money. It is not a five-, a ten-, a twenty-dollar bill.

The bank card is not money because it is not anonymous. Cash has no identification other than its value. The bank card has not only your identification number on it but also your name in two places.

The bank card is not money because its value does not exist. A dollar bill exists. The dollars backing the bank card are not there until they are spent.

The bank card is not money because it can spend more than money. Money is limited by how much there is. The card is limited only by created credit lines.

The bank card is not money because it needs a file of information in order to work. Money demands no data, it just is. Also money, itself, does not provide a way to invade your privacy. The bank card does.

The bank card is not money because it demands expensive, complex electronic systems to be practical. Money does not have to be authorized, interchanged, transmitted, encoded, captured, or billed.

The bank card is not money because you do not owe interest on your money as you spend it.

The bank card is not money because it sets up a system of worthwhile and unworthy people, dividing our society into gets and don't-gets, and cuts off the old, the unemployed, the poor.

The bank card is not money because it manufactures accelerated consumerism, encouraging people to buy faster, purchase more, use it up quicker, replace it earlier. Money can only affect the world's fixed amount of resources at a certain speed; the bank card helps eat away those fragile reserves at a perilous pace.

The bank card is not money because it contains the seeds of debt addiction, overspending, and possible personal, institutional, and community bankruptcy.

And, finally, the bank card is not money because it can make the unthinkable into a reality. Lifebank is not possible with money. It is impossible without a bank-card-type device.

The bank card really is just a 2¼"-by-3⅜" rectangle of plastic done up in numbers, letters, and kindergarten colors. Although it uses some concepts and hardware from document forms of money, it is an entirely new idea in value exchange. It should be handled just the way any new ideology or product or social revolution should be managed by us, by the legislators, by the stores, by the courts, and especially by the bankers. That is, gingerly, suspiciously, experimentally, until its value to society is proven.

The bank card is no more money than your driver's license. That is purely identification and information which says that you have passed a driving test. It does not guarantee that you are a safe driver. The bank card identifies you and says that you have passed a credit test. It does not guarantee that you are a safe spender.

If you don't use your driver's license to drive, you probably won't have an automobile crash. If you don't use your bank card to buy, you probably won't have a financial crash. Today, that is not practical. Both are needed somewhat to get places and to do things.

212

Originally, there was the bank credit card. It was a simple concept, a general neighborhood-shopping device. It gave you an unsecured line of borrowing power to use and then pay back with lengthy, high-interest installments. Then they added the feathers and ruffles. You could also get a cash advance with your card. You could use it to guarantee your checks. You could get an overdraft on your checking account. You could do most forms of simple banking with it. You could use it for birth expenses, for burial bills, and for just about everything needed for the lifetime in between.

Then it started to mutate. The "credit" card was becoming something else, to the bankers, for the bankers. People who paid their bills in full didn't have a credit card, they had a convenience card, because they weren't using the credit. Some corporations prepaid the banks a reservoir of money for their executive cards. These were not credit cards, but expense-handling cards. Cards which worked against checking accounts were not credit cards but debit cards, and if they carried overdraft privileges, then they became combination debit/credit cards. Other cards were secured by savings accounts but run through the credit card department; they were another breed.

Faced with this odd lot of cards, each of which carried different services, it was inevitable that some bankers would begin talking about one single multi-service "financial transaction" device.

That card has symbols embossed or magnetically encoded on it to tell the terminals and the electronic synapses what it can and cannot do for you. It pulls together your assorted Visa and/or MasterCard accounts into one neat, tidy file. By giving you extended financial services, credit to buy stocks, larger lines of borrowing power, major overdraft provisions, it will demand some financial security from you. That security will be noted in your file and pledged against what you spend with the card.

Beginning to sound a little bit like Lifebank? You bet your sweet assets it does.

The device called a debit card is now being pushed hard by the financial community because bankers have tardily realized that the credit card has unsolvable problems. The debit card solves those problems by immediately deducting what you just spent from what you have and charging you and the store for that service. Russell Hogg, the man who assumed control of MasterCard in 1980, described his organization's debit card as one that "looks like a credit card but works like a check." MasterCard II, as it is called, was set for a heavy 1981–82 push. Meanwhile, more than 150 members of the Visa International organization were dealing out more of their debit cards daily. Many bankers say the debit card is the light at the end of the consumer credit tunnel.

But not all bankers see the light. The disbelievers scoff, sneer, titter at the idea of EFT and Lifebank. They point out that the electronic lash-ups necessary to make it work cost too much. They say most of you would never settle for the debit card and later the more complete financial card. They say credit cards are doing just fine, even with all of their problems.

But the concept of a real Lifebank is very much alive. It may seem like fantasytime to the more conservative bankers, but some of the industry's long-range planners and leaders are still devoted to its development. Bankers who have done imaginative programs with cards, bankers who have developed extensive electronic setups, and bank card leaders who have built this baby from a mewling California infant to a brawny international heavyweight still think about it, talk about it, and subconsciously or deliberately continue to assemble the pieces that can make it workable.

With those sections jigsawed together into one practical picture, all that would be necessary for Lifebank to work is the elimination of money.

With enough persuasion from the banking industry's lobbyists, from your advertising-influenced votes, from economists, from some self-serving needs, the government would be for Lifebank. It might even legislate it into existence as a way to save the banks from themselves. With Lifebank, the government would be way ahead. It would have tighter knowledge and control of its citizenry, it could assess and collect taxes whenever it wanted to, it would have the ultimate device for controlling economic fluctuations, to handle recessions and inflations by manipulating controls on the total consumer economy.

Then all that would be needed is conversion.

There would be a week or a month or six months in which

you would turn in your cash, precious metal, checking-account balance, bonds, notes, and other assets, to a central financial office. You would be credited with the value of those belongings in your computer-located Lifebank file. Your salary and other income, from that day on, would be credited to your file through payroll and payment tapes. The unemployed and those on welfare could even receive a minimum government handout equal to the money they had been receiving. All invoices, statements, bills, and payments due would automatically be routed to your account for payment. Mortgage, car, telephone, utility, gasoline, health-plan, and other ongoing expenses would automatically be deducted every month. Every thirty days you would get a computer printout of where you stand with Lifebank and with your financial life. If you wanted to know your status in between statements, you could punch up that information on your home computer screen.

One noted banker said he "appeared" negative about Lifebank only because he knows it is a terrifying idea to us. By coming out and saying that he was definitely planning to put it into action, he could create an outcry shrill enough to shatter glass on the top floor of the Sears Tower. He also knew that, forewarned, voter-pressured legislators would probably be forced to draw up new laws to cut Lifebank off at the passbook. So, without any grand announcements or fancy hoofooraw, it could suddenly just happen. One day the credit card, then the debit card, then the transaction card, then . . . hey, look what we got here for you, folks—Lifebank.

If we do not do something, the time will come—and it is not far away—when we could all feel rich as Rockefeller but we would have little or nothing to say about what we could do with those riches. We will have lost control. Even the banks will have lost control. The Lifebank-type system will have its own reasoning, its own standards, its own momentum, its own energy, its own life; and operating without conscience, without soul, without social logic, it will also be out of control by all standards we should still live by today.

Individual bankers are people. The idea of Lifebank probably horrifies many of them when they consider it at home. They are aware of the terrifying implications and might be the first to man the street barricades against it. But something happens at work. There is a mob psychology. What is good for the bank comes first; what is good for people always follows, never leads. Humanitarianism is not a subject on meeting agendas. The welfare of people is okay so long as the welfare of the bank comes first.

Example: Bank cards. Bank cards give people more spending power for a better and more luxurious life; they identify individuals who are away from home; they help to organize personal finances. Those benefits were not dreamed up by a giving, caring financial community. What came first was the idea for small loans to the masses and the money that could be made for the bank. The golden egg came before us geese.

In some ways, the individual bankers are also being swept along by forceful financial and electronic currents. The banker who speaks up in a meeting and says, "But is it good for people?" is the banker who will suddenly find himself on the building-maintenance committee instead of the bank card one. He will not appear to have the institution's interests at heart, will not appear to be a team player. His first responsibility is to his own family, his own home, his own salary. He must either decide to go along with what is good for the bank or he will just go along, cleaning out his desk before he does.

So, Lifebank could help the government and the banks. It could solve many difficult problems for the Federal Reserve System, as well. It could also be a tidy and efficient boon to the entire business world. It could work out difficulties in the world's exchange and currency dilemmas. It could make our personal lives easier, neater, more organized, even more financially secure. It would be like having a concerned Daddy who is also a CPA supervising what we all do.

Listen, what's the loss of a little freedom compared to all of that?

What's freedom worth anyhow? Can you get a pound of it at the store, a gallon of it at a pump, a yard of it at the lumberyard? If so, what would it cost? More important, if you didn't have it, what would that cost?

If you're not willing to find out, maybe there are simple ways to cut down the bank card crisis and to postpone or even head off Lifebank.

Banks are businesses. Businesses exist to make profits. If

those profits are not being made, the business changes its products and services or fails.

The bank card is both a product and a service. Ever since the early 1960's, the huge majority of banks handling card business made profits on it, some of those profits obscenely high. Those profits came from both merchant kickbacks and from the high interest two out of three of you paid to use that bank card credit. When the 1980 credit controls were put into action, that profit dwindled. The banks were facing destructive losses which affected their entire base of financial solidity. Meanwhile, Lochinvar, in the form of the Federal Reserve Board, came out of the east to save their assets. While appearing to do something to control inflation, the Fed gave the banks a gun and a mask. That august group, which is almost above the law, set up the situation in which Hallelujah Day arrived for the banks. Under permission and even encouragement from the Fed, the banks began introducing transaction fees, higher interest rates, annual membership charges. Individually, or in combination, these new money-raising tactics were set up to dramatically increase bank card profits. Although the banks were hither and yon with them at first, the most profitable systems emerged, and those are the ones which added another cost of surviving to your cost of living.

Obviously, you can't stop using your bank card entirely. You need it today not only for those luxuries you're now used to but also just to exist.

What would happen if you cut down your bank card spending? What if you got rid of those ego-satisfying but not really necessary extra cards? What would happen if you really stopped to think how important or essential that purchase, that dinner, that trip, really is to you? You might find that a great deal of your bank card spending has been on whim, on impulse, a purchase you wouldn't have made if you had to pay with cash or check.

By thinking about your purchasing habits and about everything you buy, you may start keeping your get-it gun in its leather wallet holster, and you may find that you're not the fastest plastic in town anymore.

If enough of you did that, what would happen?

Personal debt would get smaller and more manageable. The

stores would stop buying, stocking, and pushing ridiculous luxuries you'd never consider buying for cash. The banks would actually be better off and more stable because they would not have tens of billions out in unsecured loans. The nation's economy, and even the world's, would be better off as less money chased the available goods. There would be a reduction in the inflation rate. Interest rates would also go down, because spending was not up. The Federal Reserve could get an even better rein on our bucking economy. And we would get a much-needed breathing space to decide how much of this bank card economy was worthwhile and how much should be permanently thrown out. Obviously, if everyone stopped bank card use at once, the banks and the economic structure would be in critical condition. But this will not happen. Too many people, too many businesses are now addictied to bank cards, and some form of plastic or ersatz money is here to stay. The big problems with cards can, however, be solved by dealing with the individual smaller problems of money management.

A few economists may laugh at this solution. It is too simple, they will say. Is it?

This is a financial democracy. You get to vote for what you want and against what you don't want. Manufacturers know that. Merchants know that. You vote with your money. You vote for Chevrolet over Plymouth, for Miller over Pabst, for Sears over Ward's, even for one bank over the other. Your purchasing vote counts, and counts, and counts, in the cash registers of our decision makers. If you stop voting, they stop manufacturing or selling or doing what has worked in the past and will get busy putting together or offering something you will vote for. The only reason the bank card business has become so large, and can put traditional standards, people, institutions, the marketplace, and even the state in jeopardy, is that tens of millions voted for it by blatantly using those cards. The bankers didn't do it. You and your friends did it.

You and your friends can undo it, too.

Dee Hock and other bank card spokesmen like to say that they are not forcing you to use those cards, that you are exercising the American tradition of free choice.

Fine. That works both ways. If you don't like what's going

on, if you don't like being in debt, if you don't like the dangers of personal and institutional economic collapse, if you don't like what you've read in these pages, exercise that American tradition of free choice again.

Vote against more debt, more invasion of privacy, more inflation, more dis-crediting of citizens, more theft and fraud, more unstable financial policies, more high interest, more bank profits, more rapid use of our scarce natural resources, more danger of the nightmare Lifebank becoming a reality.

All you have to do to control the bank card is not do anything.

Every time you *do not use* your bank card, you are voting against the bank card system and Lifebank.

The time has come for that.

The time for a show of hands.

Empty ones.